CHAKRAS

CHAKRAS

BALANCE YOUR BODY'S ENERGY
FOR HEALTH AND HARMONY

PATRICIA MERCIER

GODSFIELD PRESS

Dedicated to all those who walk as
Rainbows of Light in a world of shadows.

Library of Congress Cataloging-in-Publication
Data available

10 9 8 7 6 5 4 3 2 1

Published in 2000 by
Sterling Publishing Company, Inc.
387 Park Avenue South, New York, N.Y. 10016
© 2000 Godsfield Press
Text © 2000 Patricia Mercier

Patricia Mercier asserts the moral right to
be identified as the author of this work.

Designed for Godsfield Press by
The Bridgewater Book Company

Studio photography: *Ian Parsons*
Illustrations: *Graham Baker-Smith*
Picture research: *Lynda Marshall*
Page makeup/design: *Angela Neal*

Distributed in Canada by **Sterling Publishing**
c/o Canadian Manda Group,
One Atlantic Avenue, Suite 105
Toronto, Ontario, Canada M6K 3E7
Distributed in Australia by **Capricorn Link**
(Australia) Pty Ltd P O. Box 6651, Baulkham Hills,
Business Centre, NSW 2153, Australia

Every effort has been made to ensure that all the information
in this book is accurate. However, due to differing conditions,
tools, and individual skills, the publisher cannot be
responsible for any injuries, losses, and other damages that
may result from the use of the information in this book.

Printed and bound in China

ISBN 0–8069–6611–4

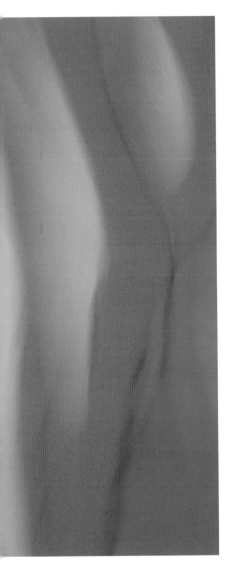

Contents

Introduction

For every one of us, life is an exploration. Yoga and meditation are central to the ancient teachings about chakras, because they open up other dimensions beyond the physical dimension. To begin to understand your chakra energies, you need to take control of your life and, most important, give yourself time just to be. Be guided by the ancient saying: "I am my own limitation—without my own limitation, I am."

Every person has a rainbowlike energy field around him or her, which is called an "aura." The aura is linked to the body by personal energy centers called "chakras." The word "chakra" originated in Sanskrit, a sacred Indian language, and means "wheel of light." This is an excellent translation, for a chakra appears to spin like a wheel or vortex and focuses the light of the aura toward the body. Auras and chakras are our "energy body."

You are not just a physical body—remarkable though that is! It is possible to sit very still and start to sense your chakras—or energy centers—in your body. When you focus intently on a part of your energy body, that area is stimulated. Some studies have shown that if you think about a particular part of your physical body too, blood flow to it increases and healing occurs more rapidly there.

Close to your skin is a measurable electromagnetic field, with an even finer, more subtle energy field stretching out, at times, to as far as 30ft (9m). With such energy around you, you can never be separate from other living things. The aura of every human, animal, plant, tree, stone, or crystal is also charged with a life-force that vibrates in harmony with cosmic and elemental energies of the universe. Whether we are with a crowd of people, or walking in a forest of tall trees, energy is received and energy is transmitted. This transmission is through our chakras: they are gathering points, drawing in information through a fine network of energy lines. For example, in a crowd of people in a supermarket, we may often absorb stress or aggression, whereas at a wedding we may feel

happiness. These feelings are derived not just from something we are hearing or seeing but also from something we are sensing with all parts of our energy body—our aura and chakras.

If we walk through a forest, our chakras are constantly communicating with the living things around us, giving messages and opening us to the natural flow of Creation. Studies have shown that trees "talk" to each other, sharing information about soil conditions, predators, rainfall, or perhaps the human being walking beneath them!

Rainbow body

Your chakras and aura can best be described as a rainbow of light. Imagine standing in your own rainbow, and begin to see how you might release your full potential for preventing disease as well as activating your spiritual development. Become responsible for yourself and understand what is right for you by listening to your "inner voice." Next time you are part of, but not central to, an emotional situation, observe which parts of your body are affected. Note what your body is sensing, beyond what you hear and see. This is an aspect of your chakras at work.

Esoteric teaching from many cultures indicates that we have 7 major chakras, 21 minor chakras, and a connecting network of energy pathways that function more readily if "nourished" by meditation, breathing exercises, and fresh food (fresh food retains life-force energy). In this book you will find many practical ways of nourishing the chakras. Most important, allow yourself time to settle into a different way of looking at the world,

> Between the top of your head and the base of your spine, there is an electrical potential of around 400 volts. This is part of the body's electromagnetic field and aura.

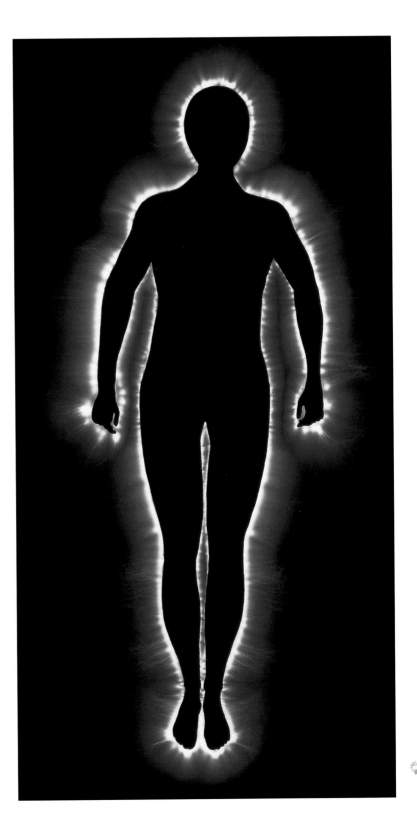

RIGHT: *The aura is created by the subtle energies surrounding the body's glowing electromagnetic field.*

then relax and explore the mysteries of the "wheels of light," as the chakras are known, for they are also the "wheels of life."

Path of knowledge

Many people, at some time in their lives, ask themselves, "Who am I?", "What is my purpose here on Earth?", or "How can I realize my full human potential?" Today, books and information technology give us an opportunity to study the wisdom and teachings of the past. By keeping an open mind, it is possible to answer some of these questions.

Piecing together myriad clues, we can follow ancient paths toward knowing ourselves, a bit like symbolically traveling a rainbow of light. A rainbow (which is clear white light split into many beautiful intense, yet subtle, colors) offers a way of knowing our inner nature, for the energies of each color have their own individual meaning, which we can learn to interpret.

This book provides practical ideas that, with the aid of visualization exercises, will enable you to begin the task of knowing your chakras, or subtle energies. You will become more radiant, vibrant, and full of life—friends will be curious to know what has changed. You do not need to be a gifted healer or clairvoyant (one who sees clearly!) to see chakras and auras. Anyone can begin to sense the power of the higher self and be able to clear blockages and revitalize the chakras, improving health, well-being, and happiness. In this way, you will find answers to your deepest questions and make your own link with the wonder of Creation.

All matter is frozen light

DAVID BOHM PHYSICIST

What are chakras?

Chakras are focused energetic life-forces. They exist within our auric field as swirling masses of color that penetrate and interact with our physical body and particularly relate to the endocrine system, central nervous system, and spine. Traditional teaching refers to the seven main chakras, or body power centers, as follows, starting from the base of the spine. Each chakra has its own color.

The sixteenth-century alchemist and physician Paracelsus wrote about a vital force that filled each person and radiated around him or her as a luminous sphere. He called this invisible force "liquor vitae," and described an "aura seminalis," made up of invisible drops, which contained an image of the whole person. This is similar to present-day holographic theories, where with a fragment of the whole, we have access to the whole.

 7. Crown chakra
Color of influence: white, violet, or gold

 6. Brow chakra (the "third eye")
Color of influence: indigo blue

 5. Throat chakra
Color of influence: turquoise (or sky blue)

 4. Heart chakra
Color of influence: green (or rose pink)

 3. Solar plexus chakra
Color of influence: yellow

 2. Sacral chakra
Color of influence: orange

 1. Root or base chakra
Color of influence: red

From this color sequence it is evident that chakras progress like colors of the light spectrum, a rainbow of muted tones, through the aura and physical body. Light is made up of waves of tiny electric and magnetic vibrations. Each color in the spectrum is a light wave of a different wavelength.

A history of energy studies

Throughout history, people have been aware of the chakras. Ancient Egyptians, the Chinese, Hindus, Zarathushtrians, Sufis, Greeks, the Maya, Native Americans, and Incas knew them as a reflection of the natural laws of the cosmos and studied them as esoteric science, giving them names such as the great powers, or the divine universal natural laws.

Eighteenth-century theories

In the early part of the 18th century, Sir Isaac Newton produced a paper on light and color, describing "electromagnetic light," "a subtle, vibrating, electric, and elastic medium," which exhibited many of the phenomena that would be explained in the electromagnetic field theories of English chemist and physicist Michael Faraday and Scottish physicist James Clerk Maxwell a century later. German industrialist and chemist Baron Karl von Reichenbach (1788–1869) also investigated electricity and magnetism. He was fascinated by the life-force that he called the "odylic force," or "Od." At the same time, American color investigator Dr. Edwin Babbitt and his inventor contemporary John Keely were studying color, light, and subtle energy.

FAR RIGHT: The seven chakras, symbolized by Sanskrit letters, show the pathway followed by prana, or life-energy, as it travels upward through the nerve channels of the body.

ABOVE: *Energy passes through the chakras like colors of the light spectrum, and creates a rainbow effect.*

ABOVE: *The aura around a saint is often depicted as a halo of golden light.*

AURA EXERCISE

You may like to try this way of seeing your own life-force light energies, which was first described by von Reichenbach. Sit in a slightly darkened room and rub your hands together vigorously. Against a dark background, stretch your arms out in front of you with your fingertips curving toward each other but not quite touching. Look to a point beyond your fingertips, without staring, and keep your gaze "soft." Most people will see very fine lines of light or colorless luminous streamers moving from and between the fingers. (If this exercise causes any eyestrain, rub your hands together again and put the palms gently over your eyes for a few minutes—this directs healing life-force from your hands to your eyes.)

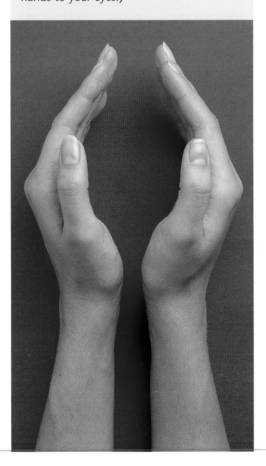

The subtle energies

This book will introduce you to a number of ideas that may be unfamiliar: aura, chakras, pathways of light, and prana (see page 12). Today we are beginning to rediscover these ancient mysteries and use them in appropriate ways for healing our minds, bodies, and souls.

THE AURA

The aura is a fluctuating, egg-shaped energy field that surrounds your body. It is made up of different layers, as listed below, starting with the one closest to your body.

• Etheric body
• Astral or emotional body
• Lower mental body
• Higher mental body
• Spiritual body
• Causal body

Information energy flows from the cosmos through the aura, and into the chakras. It also goes back out from the chakras through the aura, and into the cosmos. Think of your aura as a constantly moving rainbow of swirling colors.

ABOVE: *Auric energies interact—disruption of the emotional body can cause problems in the mental or causal body.*

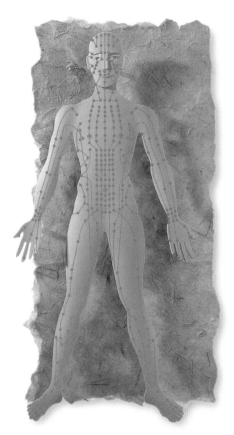

ABOVE: *Life-energy flows through channels known as meridians. Blockages in the channels can cause illness.*

PATHWAYS OF LIGHT

White light is made up of a mixture of colors called a spectrum. The seven main colors of the spectrum are red, orange, yellow, green, blue, indigo, and violet. Chakras resonate in harmony with subtle energies encoded within these seven colors. This is sometimes called our inner light. In addition, colored light flows to and from the aura via a network of fine energy channels in the body, called meridians. This is how light reaches our body cells, giving them the potent life-sustaining information that has been filtered through the aura, chakras, and energy channels.

THE CADUCEUS

In classical mythology, the flow of energy from cosmos to human was often symbolically represented by the caduceus—a staff entwined with two serpents, bearing a pair of wings at the top, which was carried by Hermes (Mercury), the messenger of the gods.

CLOAK OF MANY COLORS

Stress can cause the flow of energy around the aura and chakras to be interrupted or blocked, and illness may result. The following exercise is a good way of reducing stress. It can be used as a quick pick-me-up, or form part of a longer relaxation lasting up to 30 minutes.

Imagine wrapping yourself in a rainbow—it arcs over, caressing you with many colors that you draw closer as if enfolding yourself in a rainbow cloak. Say to yourself, "I am a being of light held in the loving embrace of Creation."

The caduceus is a symbol for the awakening of the seven chakras—its Indian connections are explained on page 25. The ancient Greek physician Asclepius used the two intertwined snakes to represent healing of both body and soul, and the symbol is still used today as the logo of the medical profession.

Early twentieth-century developments

In 1930, scientist Dr. Harold Saxton Burr studied the body's electrical field, calling it the L-field ("L" stands for "life"). In 1939, Indian Ayurvedic color doctor Dr. Col. Dinshah P. Ghadiali worked on the vibrational frequencies of colors and chakras and was far in advance of his time. Unfortunately his work with spectrochrometry (use of specific color light for healing) was not accepted by the scientific establishment. His son now promotes his theories. Austrian neuropsychiatrist Wilhelm Reich (1897–1957) investigated energy in many novel ways, calling it orgone energy, and developed a telescopelike instrument (an orgonscope) to observe it.

In London during 1908–14, Dr. Walter Kilner developed a screen coated with chemicals that enabled the aura to be seen by anyone without the faculty of clairvoyance. He wrote, "There cannot be the least doubt of the reality of the existence of an aura enveloping a human being, and this in a short time will be a universally accepted fact."

ABOVE: *The caduceus was also known as the staff of Hippocrates, named after the ancient Greek physician who was called the "Father of Medicine."*

Prana—breath of life

Prana is an Indian word meaning "life-force energy." Without it we would not be alive.

Prana gives us life in many ways: it pours into the body through our chakras and is contained in the food we eat, the water we drink, and the air we breathe. If we live close to nature, away from polluted cities, and take regular exercise, as well as eating fresh, whole foods that have neither been sprayed with chemicals, nor genetically modified in any way, and if we drink pure spring water, then we will absorb all the pranic nourishment our bodies require, and we will sparkle with vitality. But if this is not possible, we need to help ourselves to health!

In order to improve our absorption of pranic nourishment, we should eat sensibly, join a yoga or tai chi class, go out for a walk every day, and make swimming, dancing, and singing a part of everyday life. All these activities will help to move prana around in our bodies.

The Chinese refer to pranic energy as "chi." It is also sometimes known as "ki" or "qi." It moves around the body along the meridians. Free-flowing prana or chi lessens stress and increases our resistance to disease.

Prana is charged by the Earth's magnetic field and enters the body through the base chakra, setting up a resonant electromagnetic flow through the second, third, and subsequent chakras. It is carried through the body in the nervous system and in all the membranes and fluids. It flows in and around all living things.

BE POSITIVE

We need positive thought but negative ions! An ionizer will generate oxygen with a minus (negative) charge. By the ocean, or on a mountainside, air has a natural abundance of oxygen with negative ions. When we breathe in, the negative ions carry pranic life-force into the body. An excellent way of getting more negative ions into your system is to breathe deeply.

PRANIC BREATHING

When you do full pranic breathing, your body moves in a wavelike motion that can be seen as three parts of the same breath.

First, air goes right into the base of your lungs, the diaphragm pushes down on the abdominal organs, and your stomach rises.

Second, the ribs actually move apart a little as the chest rises and the stomach falls.

Third, the shoulders lift, roll back and down as the top parts of your lungs fill. As you exhale, your whole body sinks down—relaxed.

All pranic breathing is done through the nose, unless it is blocked, in which case you should endeavor to breathe in through your nose and out through your mouth.

Electromagnetics in nature—one flash of lightning discharges enough electricity into the air to power a large city for several days.

LEFT: *Sadhus, or holy men, often train in yoga and mysticism in their search for a higher state of consciousness. Their goal is to be at one with the highest spiritual power.*

BREATHING EXERCISE NO.1

Breathe only as deeply as is comfortable for you. This exercise clears blockages and activates the sacral chakra.

Sit in an upright chair, with your feet placed flat on the floor, and make sure your back is straight and comfortable.

Close your eyes, and breathe in and out as slowly and deeply as possible. Establish a rhythm to your breathing, allowing your "in" breath to last as long as your "out" breath. Count mentally to check this.

Move the palms of your hands to cover your abdomen, just below the navel, and feel movement there as you breathe. Picture a beautiful beach with the sun setting on the horizon. Imagine your sacral chakra is spinning, moving, and drawing in sunlight. Which color do you see?

As you breathe even more deeply and more slowly, picture blockages in the chakra dispersing.

Finally, imagine the sacral chakra as a beautiful, open, vibrant orange flower, then open your eyes. Rub and shake your hands.

ABOVE: *Draw the color of the setting sun into your sacral chakra and imagine the uplifting scent of sea air as you breathe deeply, peacefully releasing any energy blockages.*

Synthetic clothing materials produce electrostatic negative charges that repel beneficial negative ions. This creates an unhealthy environment for the chakras.

Light

We will be referring to light many times in this book, because each chakra has a special affinity with colored light. Also, light (as Creation) is at the core of universal spiritual teachings.

BELOW: *Each chakra is positioned at the front and back of the body, with the exception of the base chakra, which opens downward, and the crown chakra, which opens upward.*

THE ENERGY BODY IS LIGHT

Through the auric field, every chakra takes a specific energetic color of light as "nourishment," drawing it in as a spiral like water passing through a funnel. This is why healers and clairvoyants throughout the ages have been able to see the aura and chakras as swirling areas of colored light. This beautiful color and energy is fluctuating and moving all the time, like an ever-changing rainbow.

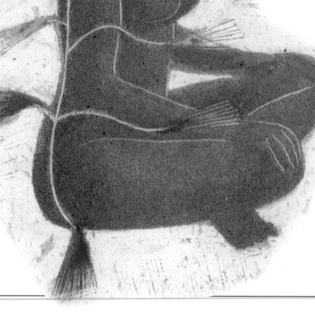

YOUR BODY IS LIGHT MADE VISIBLE

Each chakra affects different parts of the body:

The crown chakra: Mainly concerned with the cerebrum and pineal gland (which is sensitive to light levels), thus affecting the entire body.

Throat chakra: Associated with the throat, neck, thyroid and parathyroid glands, ears, windpipe, and upper part of the lungs.

Sacral chakra: Associated with the pelvis, kidneys, production of adrenaline, womb, bladder, and the sacred liquids of the body—blood, lymph, gastric juices, and sperm.

The brow or third eye chakra: Associated with the face, nose, sinuses, ears, eyes, brain functions that include the pituitary gland, cerebellum, and central nervous system.

Heart chakra: Associated with the heart, upper back, breasts, the general function of the lungs, blood and air circulation. There is a secondary chakra close to the heart chakra, which is linked to the thymus gland and the lymphatic system. It is called the thymus chakra.

Solar plexus chakra: Associated with the lower back, digestive system, liver, spleen, gall bladder, pancreas, and the production of insulin.

Base chakra: Associated with the bones, teeth, nails, gonads, anus, rectum, colon, prostate gland, blood, and blood cells.

LIGHT AND CONCEPTION

It is said that when a soul decides to incarnate on the Earth, the incoming soul selects its parents, and during conception, the upward-opening crown chakras of the parents together draw in the soul. The downward-opening base chakras receive sexual energy and the collective life-force of every living thing on Earth, which streams into the soul as it forms an embryo. Cosmic light from the stars pours through the crown chakra of the mother. Spectroscopic analysis of starlight reveals elements known on the Earth as minerals. Our physical bodies also contain minerals such as iron, magnesium, calcium, and boron. The body of each incarnating soul receives the life-force energy of the universe; human consciousness is the star-seeded jewel of life.

HEALING LIGHT

Certain healers are able to see or detect the condition of auric fields and chakras. Sometimes they even perceive disease before it manifests in the body. These healers often have the

JEWEL OF LIFE EXERCISE

Collect together a number of colored pencils or crayons (at least seven different colors) and some white paper. Sit quietly, breathing deeply and slowly. Close your eyes. Begin to imagine yourself as a jewel or crystal. Sense where your energies are focused. What colors can you see? Open your eyes and begin to draw. You may be very surprised at what's produced!

Do this exercise every week if you wish, particularly when you are working on your chakras. Keep a diary to record how your perceptions are changing.

ability of channel healing from the source of Creation to exert a beneficial influence on the chakras, allowing the body to heal itself.

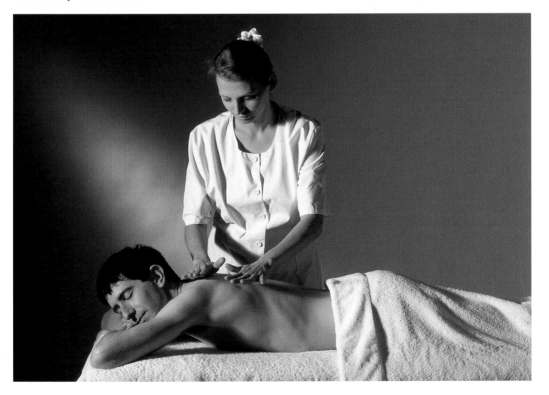

LEFT: *A sensitive healer can detect imbalances in the chakras and can channel healing light, often known as "Divine Light," directly into the affected area to restore the body's well-being.*

Major and minor chakras

We have already described the chakras as "wheels of light" or vortices of energy. As well as the seven well-known major chakras, there are 21 minor or secondary chakras. The minor chakras are associated with the following body areas: one on the sole of each foot and one behind each knee; one for each gonad, two for the spleen, one for the stomach, and one near the liver; one in the palm of each hand, one on each breast; one on each clavicle, one behind each eye, one on each temple, and one near the thymus gland.

The minor chakras could be described as the subtle energy "defenders" of the body, whereas the seven major chakras are the body's "initiators" or "guardians."

ENERGY FLOWS

The first chakra, the base, is the source of life—it is from here that the physical body is established and grows. At auric field level, the base chakra is linked to the minor chakras in the feet, knees, and gonads. This is because, in addition to energy flowing around the spinal area, energy also flows into the body through the feet and upward along the legs to the base of the spine.

The movement of energy focused through the major chakras is primarily associated with the endocrine glands, which secrete hormones, stimulating the physiological processes.

The minor, secondary chakras connect with the lymphatic vascular system. This carries excess fluid and unwanted waste particles from body cells, helping the body to fight disease and infections.

THE ALTA MAJOR CHAKRA

This chakra is situated at the base of the back of the skull and is concerned with memory traces and survival patterns inherited from our prehistoric ancestors.

THYMUS CHAKRA

This is one of the minor chakras, but it is also important in its own right as an emerging energy center, with a specialized ability to

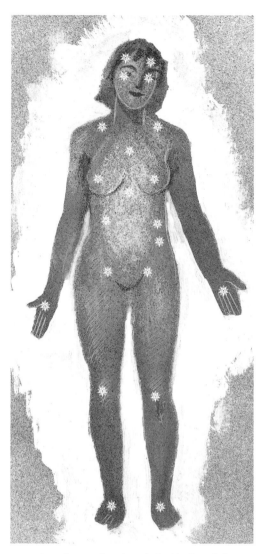

ABOVE: *A good energy flow through the 21 minor chakras helps to detoxify the physical body, defending it against infection. Those behind the knee, in the groin, and near the clavicle are positioned near waste-removing lymph nodes.*

combat attack by environmental pollutants and invading viruses. Its resonant color is pale pink or pale blue.

CHAKRA BALANCE

Each chakra has certain powers and qualities enabling it to negotiate with or balance adjacent chakras. For example, the throat chakra is concerned with all types of

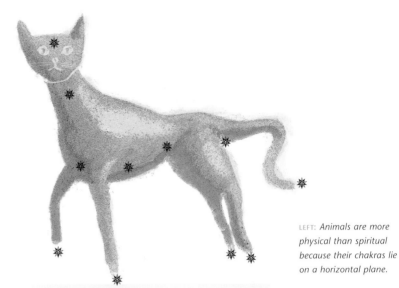

communication, and if you have already developed unconditional love activity (see page 95) in the heart chakra, and both chakras are activated you will speak with loving passion. If the brow chakra has been activated, your voice will reflect higher level insights. Specific body areas are also activated by each chakra (see page 14).

ANIMALS

Animals have chakras too. Their lower chakras are more active than a human's, and their crown chakras are different because their spines are horizontal and they do not develop spiritually as humans do. Interestingly, compared to a dog, a cat's paw chakras and third eye chakra are very active and finely developed.

LEFT: Animals are more physical than spiritual because their chakras lie on a horizontal plane.

CHAKRA QUALITIES

Here are the positive chakra qualities that flow and assist one another:

Chakra	Power
1 Base	Stabilizing; vitality; root of collective unconscious
2 Sacral	Purifying; joy; feminine principle; receptivity to nature
3 Solar plexus	Transforming knowledge; masculine principle; solar/cosmic force
4 Heart	Balancing; unconditional love; compassion; healing
5 Throat	Transmitting; creative self-expression; communication
6 Brow	Insight and intuition
7 Crown	Transcending; wisdom; universal consciousness

THYMUS CHAKRA RECHARGING EXERCISE

If you wish to use an essential oil vaporizer in the room while you do this exercise, add four drops of pure lavender oil and two drops of thyme oil to the water in the vaporizer. This will assist breathing.

Breathe in gently and slowly, visualizing your breath as a beautiful soft pink or lavender color. Imagine the breath becoming focused between the heart and throat chakras at the center of your chest, and gradually allow a picture of a hazy field of lavender to form in your mind's eye. Picture yourself lying on the ground among the flowers. Continue breathing in this way for no more than five minutes.

BELOW: Visualization can recharge your chakras. Imagine the color of the chakra in a natural scene. For example, lavender is the resonant color of the thymus chakra.

The Indian tradition

Yoga, a Sanskrit word meaning "union" or "joining," is a system of Indian philosophy that combines three aspects of our life-energy—the physical, the mental, and the spiritual. Its techniques train the body and the mind through exercise, good diet, relaxation, and meditation. Deep breathing exercises control the flow of prana, or life-force, through the chakras.

The physical postures, or "asanas," and the mental and spiritual training undertaken in yoga promote physical and spiritual well-being. The development and function of the chakras in controlling the flow of prana is of primary importance in yogic tradition. Our knowledge of chakras is drawn from some of the most ancient written texts in the world, including the *Hathapradipika*, the *Yoga Sutras* of Patanjali, and the *Bhagavad Gita*. Yoga postures, relaxation, and meditation safely activate the chakras. Anyone, of any age or physical ability, can learn relaxation techniques and/or practice some form of yoga.

THE INDIAN TRADITION OF CHAKRAS

All chakras are depicted with a certain number of petals, which correspond to the number of nadis emanating from them. Nadis are nerve channels in the astral body (see page 24).

CHAKRA	PETALS	ENDOCRINE GLAND	CEREBROSPINAL LEVEL	SENSE	YOGA POSTURE
1 BASE Muladhara	4	Testes/ovaries	Coccygeal	Smell	Padmasana
2 SACRAL Svadisthana	6	Adrenals	Sacral	Taste	Paschimotanasana
3 SOLAR PLEXUS Manipura	10	Pancreas	Lumbar	Sight	Bhujangasana
4 HEART Anahata	12	Thymus	Thoracic	Touch	Virabhadrasana
5 THROAT Vishudda	16	Thyroid/parathyroids	Cervical	Hearing	Halasana and Matsyasana
6 BROW Anja	2 or 96	Pituitary	Brain stem	ESP	Nataraja asana
7 CROWN Sahasrara	1,000 or 972	Pineal	Fore brain	All	Bakasana and Sirasana

RIGHT: *A Hindu devotee sits in an asana, or yogic pose. The seven chakras are visible along the center of his body.*

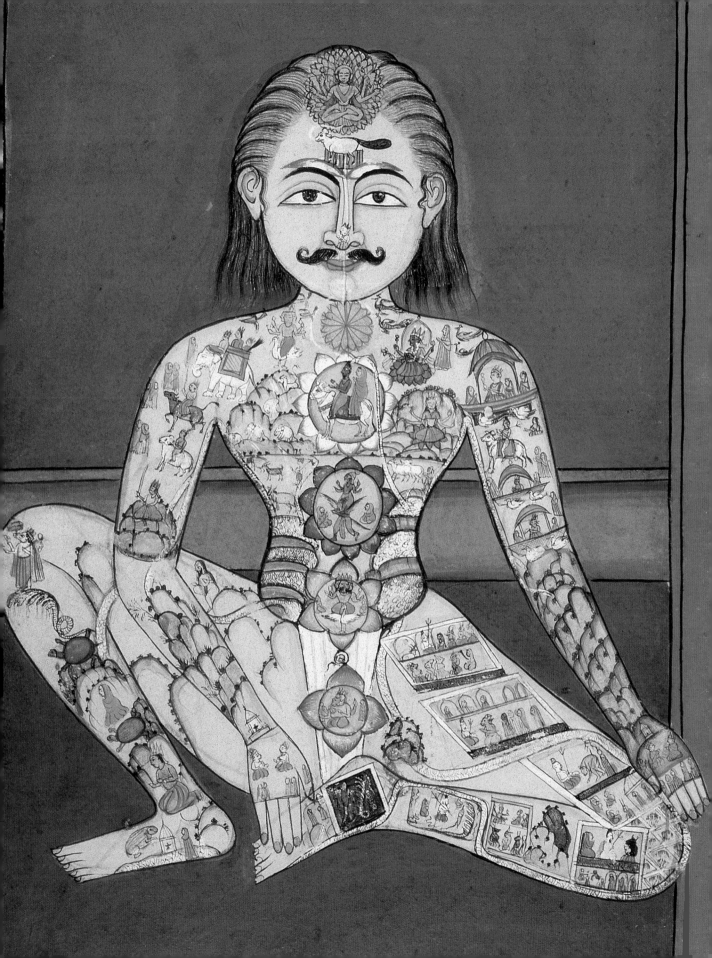

Relaxation and meditation

Steady, keeping body, head and
Neck upright and still, having
Directed his gaze to the front
Of his nose, without looking in any direction.

BHAGAVAD GITA CH. 6, V.13

LEFT: *The Hindu god Vishnu, preserver and healer of the universe, holds a chakra in one of his four hands to symbolize the wheel of time.*

BELOW: *Yogis smear their bodies with consecratory ashes, which are believed to contain the divine presence and avert evil.*

Relaxation methods are modern-day survival techniques, which are best learned when you are not under a lot of stress. When stressed we find all sorts of reasons for not starting to change! But if we don't recognize and deal with stress, the cumulative effects of it can be disastrous for our health. A relaxed body is a prerequisite for meditation. If the body is still, the mind follows. When the mind is still, meditation begins.

RELAXATION EXERCISE NO. 1

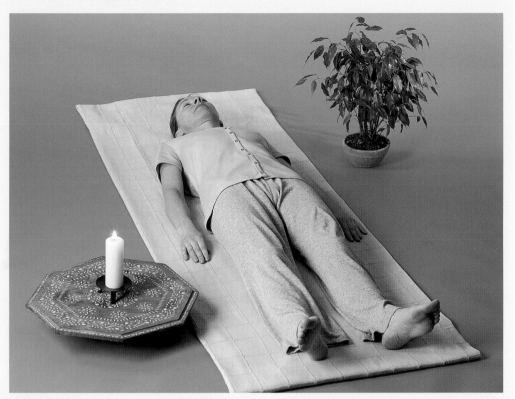

A few minutes spent gently pounding the tops of your shoulders with your fists will release tension in the head and neck.

This exercise is based on yoga techniques. It's a good idea to record the exercise on a cassette tape, beginning and ending with some beautiful soft music. Ensure you are somewhere you will not be disturbed, and unplug your telephone. Spread a blanket on the floor to lie on. This relaxation takes up to 30 minutes and is practiced in the position known as *Shavasana*.

1 Lie flat on your back with your feet slightly apart. If you have a back problem, bend your knees but keep your feet flat on the blanket about 2½ft (0.75m) apart, and support your knees with cushions. Close your eyes. Take three deep breaths, and breathe out any feelings of stress each time you exhale.

2 Starting with your right foot, relax it, then proceed to relax your right leg, muscle by muscle, all the way up. Now do the same with your left foot and leg.

3 Relax your buttocks, sexual organs, pelvis, and lower back. Relax your solar plexus area, heart, and lungs.

4 Starting from the base of your spine, let each vertebra settle into a relaxed position, traveling right up your neck. Experience waves of relaxation washing over you.

5 Feel your arms and hands becoming limp and heavy. Move your head gently from side to side to release any tension in the neck. Relax all the muscles of your face and scalp, and finally allow the activity in your brain to slow down.

6 Let the soft music you are playing gently float over you. Try not to go to sleep, but maintain a state of relaxed awareness. When the music finishes, slowly start to breathe more deeply, stretch your legs, then your arms, roll onto one side, and sit up. Be gentle with yourself for the rest of the day!

Chakras and the elements

*That yogi is said to be united who
Is contented in knowledge and
Experience, unshakeable, master of
The senses, who is balanced in
Experiencing earth, stone, or gold.*

BHAGAVAD GITA, CH.6, V.8

The chakras need to be kept in balance for optimum physical, mental, and spiritual health. Sometimes chakras are referred to as "closed" or "open." It's more correct to describe them as active or passive, because this better reflects the movement of energy through them. Different types of natural elemental energy provide "food" for the chakras. Recognizing their qualities makes it much easier to balance the chakras. Also, if you use a relaxation exercise you will, with practice, be able to sense whether your chakras are receptive to the flow of natural elemental energy.

The elements

There are four main elements—Earth, Water, Fire, and Air—plus Ether and Spirit. Each element has its own character, strengths, and other qualities. Each of the seven chakras is associated with one of these elements.

You can work with the elements to help clear blockages in the chakras caused by the unnatural conditions imposed by the bustle of daily life. By clearing chakra blockages, you enhance your potential for spiritual development. Do not think of the elements as abstract ideas—esoteric teaching gives them form, as gods, goddesses, or beings.

> Fire, through a process called moxibustion, is used in the East to release stagnant energy in the meridians. To help this process, a burning stick of mugwort herb is held close to the skin.

Earth Elementals: Beings who live in and through the Earth dimension, such as gnomes, fairies, trolls, gods and goddesses, and beings of the crystals, trees, and mountains. Work with these energies aids development of the base chakra, which is associated with the Indian element of *Prithivi*.

Water Elementals: Beings who live in and through the Water dimension, such as undines (water spirits), guardians of sacred wells and springs, and river gods and goddesses. These elementals are linked to the sacral chakra, the sacred waters of our bodies, and the Indian element of *Apas*.

Fire Elementals: Beings who live in and through the Fire dimension, such as salamanders and keepers of sacred flames. Understanding the fire elementals benefits the solar plexus chakra, assists transmutation and assimilation of food into color/light/pranic energy, and helps appreciation of the Indian element of *Tejas*.

Air Elementals: Beings who live in and through the Air dimension: sylphs, and gods and goddesses associated with mountaintops. Recognition of these energies fulfills our heart/ lung connection, develops the heart chakra, and the Indian element of *Vayu*.

These four elementals—Earth, Water, Fire, and Air—work through the first four chakras. Above the heart chakra, our chakras resonate more with the spiritual realms than the elemental. The Indian words associated with the spiritual realms are *Akasha* (space), *Kala* (time), *Dik* (direction in space), and *Atman* (soul).

BELOW: *The elements of Earth, Water, Fire, and Air can have grounding, cleansing, empowering, and balancing effects.*

RELAXATION EXERCISE NO. 2

As with the first relaxation exercise, you may like to record this routine on a cassette tape, beginning and ending with some soft music. Be somewhere you will not be disturbed and turn off your telephone. Lie on a blanket of natural fibers, specially kept for these exercises.

1 First of all adopt the relaxation pose described on page 21, getting your body into a completely relaxed state.

2 Focus on the area of your base chakra and legs. Through your feet you are closely connected with the Earth—allow the strength and energy of the Earth element to flow upward to clear any blockages in the base chakra. Visualize the color bright red while doing this.

3 Focus on the area of your second chakra (the sacral chakra). Think about drawing the cleansing power of Water through this chakra to clear any blockages. Visualize the color orange while you are doing this, together with an image of a crescent Moon above the ocean.

4 Focus on the area of your third chakra (the solar plexus chakra). Through this chakra you can connect with the positive energies of the Sun—feel yourself drawing in the power of Fire to clear any blockages. Visualize the color bright yellow while doing this.

5 Focus on the area of your fourth chakra (the heart chakra). Through this chakra you can draw into your heart the freedom and empowerment of the Air element to clear any blockages. Imagine you are doing this, and at the same time visualize a soft green color.

6 Allow the elemental quality of Spirit to flow upward from your heart chakra to the top of your head, clearing any blockages. Visualize a clear golden-white light doing this.

When you are ready to finish your relaxation, begin to breathe a little more deeply for about five minutes. Deeper breathing integrates the elements of Earth, Water, Fire, Air, and Spirit in your body. Return to usual consciousness and slowly sit up.

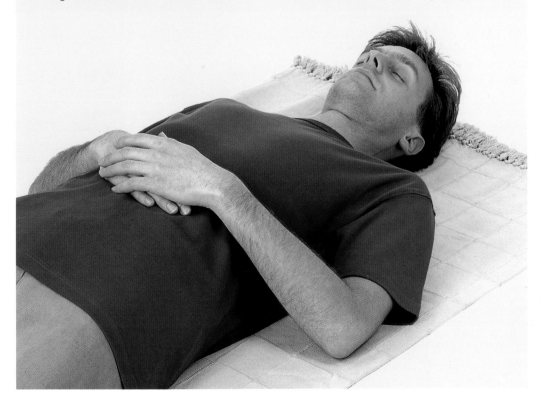

The energy pathways

According to yogic tradition, within our subtle energy fields there are 72,000 energy channels called "nadis," which connect the aura and chakras with our physical body. Some of these channels, or meridians, are used in acupuncture. Yoga and meditation address three nadis considered to be the primary channels, in order to purify them and enable life-force, or prana, to flow freely.

• **Ida nadi:** The left or lunar channel, connected to the right side of the brain, flowing down to the base of the spine.

• **Pingala nadi:** The right or solar channel, connected to the left side of the brain, flowing down to the base of the spine.

• **Sushumna nadi:** The great central nadi, connected to the spine and the central nervous system.

The Ida and Pingala nadis cross and recross the Sushumna at the seven chakra points, and meet at the brow chakra, bringing a spiral of energy through the body, centered around the spine.

Types of yoga

Traditionally, the following types of yoga are used to bring each chakra to peak performance.

• Hatha and Kundalini yoga for the first chakra (*Muladhara*).
• Bhakti yoga for the second chakra (*Svadisthana*).
• Tantra yoga for the third chakra (*Manipura*).
• Karma yoga for the fourth chakra (*Anahata*).
• Mantra yoga for the fifth chakra (*Vishudda*).
• Jnana and Yantra yoga for the sixth chakra (*Ajna*).
• The practice of all the types of yoga just mentioned activates the seventh chakra (*Sahasrara*), and transcendental consciousness occurs spontaneously.

Whichever type of yoga you practice, chakras must always be activated upward, from the base to the head. This ensures that personal growth is grounded (with the element of Earth) and balanced first at the base chakra.

> The innermost part of the human brain produces 1 pint (600ml) of cerebral spinal fluid a day and is known by yogis as the Sunya Desha, or Source of the Radiant Ether.

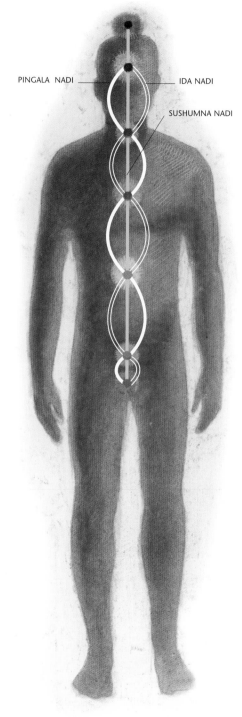

PINGALA NADI — IDA NADI

SUSHUMNA NADI

ABOVE: *Prana curves in and out along two of the three main nadis, or energy channels, crossing and recrossing the central Sushumna nadi at each of the chakra points as it rushes upward on its path through the physical body.*

With his being deep in peace,
Freed from fear, settled in the vow
Of chastity, with mind subdued
And thought given over to Me,
Let him sit united
Realizing Me as the Transcendent.

BHAGAVAD GITA CH. 6, V.14

Kundalini—the serpent fire

At the base chakra is the "coiled serpent" of Kundalini—the sexual urge, and our primary means of sensing life. In the East, Tantric practices have been developed to move sexual energy from base to higher chakras. Yoga moves the "Serpent Fire" slowly through the chakras. In the first chakra, it increases our connection to nature and enhances our sex life. In the second, it enhances understanding of others. In the third, it improves assimilation of nourishment. In the fourth, it boosts heart function and the ability to feel love. In the fifth, it enables us to express ourselves. In the sixth, it enhances creativity. In the seventh chakra, it improves our ability to sleep and experience altered states of consciousness. The next stage is ecstatic spiritual experience.

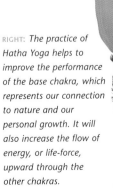

RIGHT: *The practice of Hatha Yoga helps to improve the performance of the base chakra, which represents our connection to nature and our personal growth. It will also increase the flow of energy, or life-force, upward through the other chakras.*

BREATHING EXERCISE NO. 2

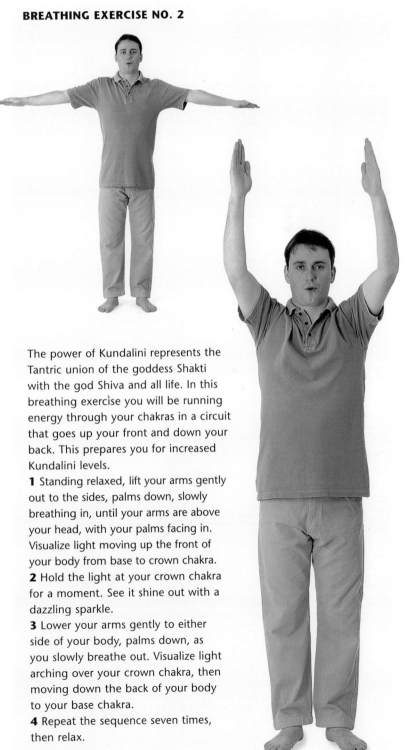

The power of Kundalini represents the Tantric union of the goddess Shakti with the god Shiva and all life. In this breathing exercise you will be running energy through your chakras in a circuit that goes up your front and down your back. This prepares you for increased Kundalini levels.

1 Standing relaxed, lift your arms gently out to the sides, palms down, slowly breathing in, until your arms are above your head, with your palms facing in. Visualize light moving up the front of your body from base to crown chakra.
2 Hold the light at your crown chakra for a moment. See it shine out with a dazzling sparkle.
3 Lower your arms gently to either side of your body, palms down, as you slowly breathe out. Visualize light arching over your crown chakra, then moving down the back of your body to your base chakra.
4 Repeat the sequence seven times, then relax.

Keeping your chakras healthy

Our chakras and aura carry a blueprint of information from the cosmos. They are like a mold, or pattern, into which life pours itself. But if we are exposed to pollution or infections, our chakras struggle to remain healthy. It is at these times that we can do much to help ourselves by chakra visualization exercises and positive thoughts. Dwell for a moment on the old saying: "as we think—so we become."

SIGNS OF TROUBLE

From time to time many of us have frittered away our time, flitting from one inconsequential thing to another, filling our minds with much trivia that we could easily discard. Stress levels rise if we become fixed in these ways of living, and little telltale signs of complaint from the body start to occur, such as general weakness or lethargy, difficulty in digesting certain foods, frequent mood swings, bags under the eyes, and depression and/or irritability. These can be early indications that subtle pranic energies entering through your chakras are not keeping up with the rate at which your style of life is discharging them. Consequently you may experience food allergies, cravings for alcohol, cigarettes, candies, chocolate, and processed foods, muscle cramps, problems with yeast infections (candida), fingernails that break easily, and hair in poor condition. As the body's resources become more and more depleted, you may succumb to frequent bouts of illness. At this point it is critical that you supplement orthodox allopathic medical treatment with "energy medicine."

ENERGY MEDICINE

"Energy medicine" is an overall term used to describe therapies and complementary practices that move and increase energy to enhance the health of the body. Complementary therapies are generally holistic (meaning that they treat the whole person) and have a beneficial effect on the aura and chakras. The following therapies restore balance to the chakras, and also work on specific levels of the aura.

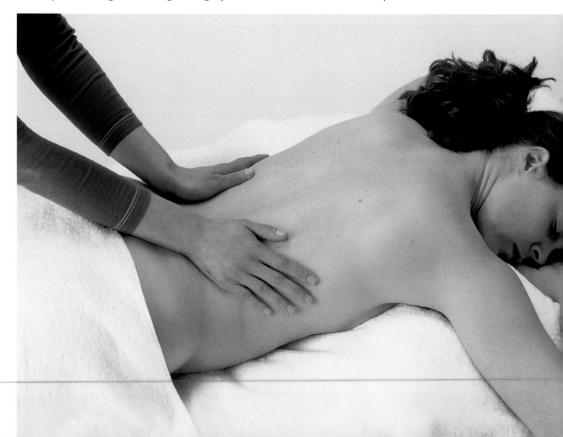

RIGHT: *Massage benefits the base chakra, which draws energy into the body and sends it upward along the spine.*

THERAPIES THAT BENEFIT THE CHAKRAS

First chakra, and the connection to the physical body: osteopathy, chiropractic, homeopathy, massage.

Second chakra and etheric levels of the aura: tai chi, yoga, shiatsu, herbalism, acupuncture.

Third chakra and emotional levels of the aura: counseling, affirmations, relaxation techniques, intuitive aromatherapy massage, flower essences.

Fourth chakra and mental level of the aura: meditation, color light therapy, crystal healing.

Fifth chakra and higher mental level of the aura: gem elixirs, toning sounds, metamorphic technique (working on the spinal reflexes of feet, hands, and head that relate to a person's pre-natal period), radionics (holistic energy healing).

Sixth chakra and spiritual level of the aura: Reiki (a form of "hands-on" energy healing) and all forms of spiritual healing.

Seventh chakra: transcendental meditation. The seventh chakra cannot be fully activated unless the other six chakras are balanced. Please note: this is a guide, not a definitive list.

FINDING A HOLISTIC PRACTITIONER

Holistic practitioners treat not just the physical symptoms but the whole person, physically, emotionally, and spiritually. There are now many complementary/holistic health practices—look in your local area. When first visiting practitioners, always ask whether they belong to a professional body with a code of practice, and ask to see their qualifications and certificate of insurance.

LEFT: Herbalism benefits the sacral chakra, which affects our ability to assimilate nutrition from our diet and our emotional life.

STRESS RELEASE EXERCISE

Practice this exercise before you actually need it. These three de-stressing breaths can be used to defuse a difficult situation. If you have a large mirror, watch yourself while doing the exercise.

1 Stand and face a mirror. Imagine a situation that often causes you stress, and keep thinking about it. Tense your muscles all over for a minute, clenching your fists and lifting your shoulders, and make your face scowl.

2 Breathe in, and stop thinking about the stressful situation. Hold your breath for a moment, then breathe out through your mouth. Relax your shoulders.

3 Take a second breath, hold it, then breathe out through your mouth. Relax your arms and hands.

4 Take a third breath, hold it, then breathe out through your mouth. Relax the rest of your body.

5 Smile!

6 Breathe more slowly than normal for a few minutes, then start to move gently.

7 During the rest of the day, check at regular intervals that your tension has not returned.

He whose self is
*   established in Yoga,*
Whose vision
*   everywhere is even,*
Sees the Self
*   in all beings,*
And all beings
*   in the Self.*

BHAGAVAD GITA
CH.6, V.29

Seeing the subtle energies

If you have just rushed home from work or the supermarket, it won't be the best time to see energies! You need to prepare yourself first. Follow the ideas on this page. Use them as often as you wish, for practice is the key to success.

HOW TO SENSE THE SUBTLE ENERGIES

Preparation

Take a shower—this cleans and tightens up your auric field. Switch off telephones and electrical equipment. Sit down in a quiet place and practice pranic breathing (see page 25). The aim is to slow down brain function to one of quiet calm. The state you achieve is similar to deep relaxation and prepares you for meditation.

RIGHT: *Chakra energy can be sensed by placing the palms inside the body's auric field.*

Intention

Affirm that you want to see the aura for good reasons; if you think of it as a party game, it won't work. If you are following a regular spiritual practice of some kind, yoga or meditation, it is likely that your ability to see energy will develop as a matter of course.

Seeing the aura

In a dimly lit room, stand in front of a dark background and look into a mirror. Keep looking beyond your image with a "soft" gaze. You may start to see your energy field.

If working with a friend, have the person stand in front of a dark background and look past him or her with a "soft" gaze. Once you have learned to see an aura in this way, you may observe colors moving around or spiral flows of chakras. Whatever you do, don't get anxious if it doesn't happen immediately. Anxiety will cause brainwaves to jump back to normal levels of activity.

Sensing the chakras

To sense the chakras, you use the palms of your hands to "scan" over a friend's body without touching it. Keep your hands about about 5in (13cm) away from the body's surface. You may feel, but not see, different types of energies—they may be hot, cold, pulsating, or stagnant. Don't chat as you do the scanning, or the subtle energy signals will not be sensed. When you have finished, shake your hands vigorously to release any unwanted energies, then change roles.

DOWSING RODS

The traditional process of finding water by using a hazel twig is called dowsing. Subtle energies can also be detected by using two L-shaped metal rods. Many people make rods from a bent piece of metal wire about 18in (46cm) long— wire cut from coathangers is ideal.

By holding a rod in each hand you can find the energy fields of plants, humans, and animals. You just have to ask a specific question, such as: "Show me the edge of the cat's aura" —and the rods (which had been held pointing

ENERGY EXERCISE

Sit opposite a friend. Hold the palms of your hands up to each other without touching. What can you feel? It may be a warm sensation or tingling. Next, both shut your eyes. One of you becomes the "giver" and one the "receiver" of energy. What can you feel now? Is it different if you are giving or receiving? You may sense that the energy from your partner's hands is pushing or pulling. Perhaps you are really sensitive and can pick up the emotional state of your friend, or perhaps you feel nothing the first time you try it. Practice with different people to experience various kinds of energy. Always wash your hands in cold water when you have finished, so that you don't hold on to your friend's energy.

In Europe, *virgula divina* (divining rods) have been used for dowsing since the Middle Ages.

forward) will spontaneously move outward as the edge of the cat's auric field is reached. You can also ask where chakras are.

Protecting your chakras

Some people can take your energy away—they are a bit like energy vampires. They crave more energy for themselves and the only way they know to get it is to "steal" it—they haven't learned any of the good ways to increase energy shown in this book. If you are going into a difficult situation with another person or group, you can very quickly protect your chakras by mentally wrapping a cloak of light around you. Start at the top, above your head, and draw it around in an egg shape, reaching right down to the ground. Nobody will know you are doing it, but you will feel a lot better.

CHAKRA PROTECTION EXERCISE

Whenever you are doing any energy work, you should finish in the following way.

If you have been meditating on your own, imagine that all your chakra energies are represented by the petals of a flower. When your inner experience is complete, visualize the petals of each chakra closing one by one until the flower is closed and at rest.

If you have been doing healing work with a friend, prepare each chakra for normal energy flows by visualizing drawing a circle of light around it (or indicating a circle with the forefinger without touching the body), then seal it with a cross, a pentagram, or another positive symbol of your own spiritual practice.

ABOVE: *Rudolf Steiner believed that enhanced human consciousness can perceive spiritual worlds independent of the senses.*

The influence of life cycles

He is never born, nor does he ever die;
Nor once having been, does he cease to be.
Unborn, eternal, everlasting, ancient.
He is not slain when the body is slain.

BHAGAVAD GITA CH.2, V.20.

This verse from the Bhagavad Gita, an ancient epic text from India, tells of great cycles of ever-lasting human development from before birth to beyond death. Within all life on this planet are cycles of development from those of the tiniest organisms, the microcosm, to cycles of influence from our Moon, Sun, and planets. One such cycle is the 28-day female menstrual cycle, which corresponds to 13 Moons in a solar year.

THE SACRED SEVEN

Life cycles lasting seven years have been described in various schools of spiritual development. Rudolf Steiner, an Austrian artist, mystic, and seer who founded Anthroposophy (inspired study of the spiritual essence of human and cosmos) in 1913, believed that understanding seven-year cycles of human growth was fundamental to our development. Yogic teaching also links the seven sacred chakras to seven-year periods, commencing at

birth in the base chakra and working successively upward through each of the chakras. In our fiftieth year we begin another seven-year cycle, starting at the base chakra, but at a higher "vibration" of energy and consequently a higher learning experience. In addition, each year within the seven-year periods is influenced by successive chakras.

Use the charts opposite as follows. For example, at the completion of the fourth year of life (coming up to the fourth birthday) the overall influence comes from the first (base) chakra (chart 1) with yearly influence from the color green (chart 2). So this is a time in a child's development when loving security is vital in order to be able to begin loving relationships. By the time the child is in his fifth year, loving security enables greater expression and vocalization of loving care to others.

Another example: A person coming up to her fortieth birthday will be under the seven-year influence of the sixth (brow) chakra (chart 1), with the year "colored" by the energy of turquoise (chart 2). Therefore, the fortieth year should be a time of inner personal tuition, moving energy from concerns of the physical body to the development of higher chakra energy of the fifth (throat) chakra (chart 2) through intuitive communication with others.

RIGHT: *This seventeenth-century manuscript shows the new Moon waxing into a full Moon (at the bottom) and waning until its rebirth at the next new Moon. Earth energies ebb and flow with its phases.*

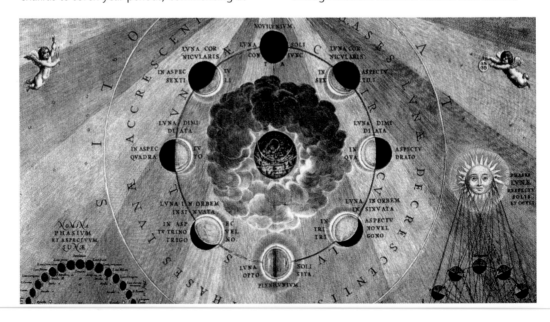

CHART ONE: BASIC UNDERSTANDINGS WITHIN EACH SEVEN YEAR CYCLE

YEAR	CHAKRA CYCLE	KEY WORDS
0–7 and 50–56	First	Life-force energy. Connection to the Earth and material world. Stability.
8–14 and 57–63	Second	Sensuality. Creativity. Enthusiasm. Exploration.
15–21 and 64–70	Third	Development of personality and feelings. Wisdom.
22–28 and 71–77	Fourth	Love. Compassion. Selflessness. Development of healing skills in self and others.
29–35 and 78–84	Fifth	Communication. Self-expression. Inspiration. Independence. Open to higher development.
36–42 and 85–91	Sixth	Realization of inner senses, for example, clairvoyance, Intuition. Responsibility.
43–49 and 92–98	Seventh	Time of inner work. Unity. Enlightenment.

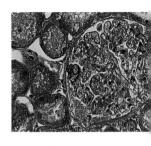

ABOVE: *Biologically, every seven years we are renewed. Within that time, every one of our body cells is replaced by a new one.*

CHART TWO: BASIC UNDERSTANDINGS WITHIN EACH ONE-YEAR CYCLE

Each year is "colored" in the following way, in a repeating spiral of development:

First year of life: red energy primordiality, invigoration, action

Second year of life: orange energy exploration, creativity

Third year of life: yellow energy expansion, limitless possibility

Fourth year of life: green energy love, expression of inner goodness

Fifth year of life: turquoise energy protection, communication

Sixth year of life: indigo blue energy deepening experience

Seventh year of life: violet energy inner transition and contemplation

Chakras in other cultures

We have seen how chakra teachings were developed within the Indian yogic system, providing an acceptance of subtle energy in everyday life. Many other cultures around the world also refer to chakras.

ZARATHUSHTRIANISM

This teaching from the Middle East, said to be 9,000 years old, still exists in India. It was called Zoroastrianism when it was the national religion of Iran. Zarathushtrian priest-doctors cite 16 main chakras located within the aura, which are connected to the physical organs and brain. The chakras are "fed" with cosmic energy from the 27 visible constellations of stars. Light force (called *Athre*) comes from the stars and goes through the forcefield of our solar system, past the outer planets to Jupiter, from where it is transmitted to the inner force-field of our Sun, Mars, Venus, and Mercury, then to the Earth and human chakras.

THE MAYA OF CENTRAL AMERICA

The Maya refer to chakras as the great powers. A chakra is often seen on their carvings of human figures—depicted as an "O" with another circle inside. This is called "ol," or knowledge and consciousness. Often the heart chakra is marked with a "G," or spiral, representing the Milky Way or "egg essence" from which we originate and

ABOVE: *Followers of the Iranian prophet Zoroaster (c.628–c.551 BCE) believed that cosmic energy traveled from the universe directly into humans, vitalizing their chakras.*

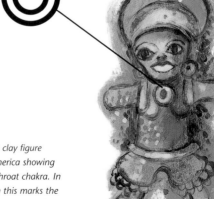

RIGHT: *A Mayan clay figure from Central America showing an "O" at the throat chakra. In Mayan tradition this marks the place where the energy of spirit-consciousness is centered.*

ABOVE: *Exiled Tibetan Buddhists meet for evening prayer in Dharamsala, India. The Tibetans preserved many Sanskrit texts by translating them before the originals were lost.*

to which we return after death. According to Valmiki, an Indian sage, the Naga Maya brought their culture to India in 2700 BCE. Manetho, an Egyptian priest, reported that Mayan teachings spread to other parts of Asia and Africa. The Maya say our bodies are sacred temples that integrate the seven great powers of light through the chakras in the form of a winding serpent. Some Mayan and Indian words are similar: Chakra (Indian) and Chacla (Mayan), and Kundalini (Indian) and Kultanlilni (Mayan).

THE TIBETANS

Tibetan mystical Buddhists refer to the aura as "the rainbow of liberated energy" and assign five colors to the chakra elements of Earth, Water, Fire, Ether, and Spirit (although within their calendars and acupuncture systems they use the Eastern concept of elements).

WESTERN MYTH AND LEGEND

Medieval writings and paintings depicted the dragon as a metaphor for sexual energy that needed to be controlled or even "killed"—for example, in the story of St. George, who thrust a sword through a dragon to pin it to the ground. The fearsome dragon represented the powerful sexual drive of the first chakra, and the sword was in reality a sword of light, the channel of energy through which sexuality could be transmuted.

In Arthurian myths, stories about the Knights of the Round Table and their quest for the Holy Grail include deeply hidden esoteric teachings about the chakras. The knights undertake many adventures that activate the lower chakras as the story moves toward the Grail cup or chalice, a symbol that represents the heart chakra. The plot revolves around asking a question in order to be shown the purity of the Grail mass. When a knight asks the right question, the flow of energy at his throat chakra is unlocked. As a consequence, an inner vision is activated in the brow chakra, which gives every witness of the Grail mass a different insight, providing him with spiritual "food" that he most desires. This nourishment descends from above through the crown chakra and fills the chalice of his heart.

In Crete and Egypt, the bumblebee symbolized the Mother Goddess and the first chakra. As enlightened beings, Egyptian pharaohs wore a cobra on their headdresses to show that Kundalini had risen to their higher chakras.

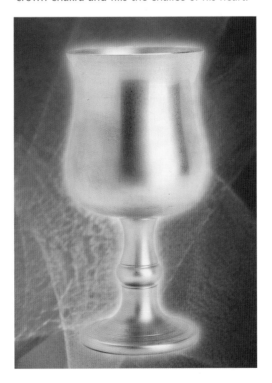

LEFT: *In European legend, the quest for the Holy Grail symbolized the search for a mystical union with God.*

The chakra rainbow

In this chapter, each chakra is looked at in depth, providing a practical basis for further understanding. Inspirational pictures and meditations enable you to visualize your own chakras in many different ways. An affirmation is given in each section: this is a short sentence of words of wisdom used to focus the mind away from everyday thoughts. You may repeat it silently to yourself.

ABOVE AND RIGHT:
Just as the shape of a lotus changes under the influence of light, a chakra can be open (active) or closed (passive) to the passage of life-energy.

Note: When you practice the meditational visualizations in this chapter, please ensure that you are somewhere where you will not be disturbed for at least half an hour, and unplug your telephone. You might like to record the words on a cassette tape, beginning and ending with calming music.

Although you can't normally see chakras, their effects are profound. If you practice meditational visualizations, awareness of your chakra energies will increase. You will be able to sense why you feel the way you do and you will also know which chakra requires "strengthening."

Chakra growth and nourishment

The body needs four basic sources of "nourishment"—food for growth, water for metabolism, air to breathe, and electrical or fire energy (including energy that passes along the nerves of the physical body, and prana, which flows through the chakras and aura).

Colors in our aura reflect spiritual life changes as we grow from infant to adult. In the first seven years of life, auric colors are developing in intensity. As a child grows, the colors of light passing through the chakras should remain balanced. However, chakra energy can be depleted or blocked by a lack of "nourishment," or other problems. To pre-empt the physical manifestation of disease, it's important to reduce harmful influences such as poor diet, pollution, and an overreliance on prescription drugs.

When the seventh seven-year cycle is completed, around about age 49 (see page 31), there begins a transition from the need to have a strongly active sexual life. The desire for materialistic possessions may lessen as incoming cosmic energy begins a transformative process through the higher chakras above the heart. As this occurs, a refinement and lightening of colors is observable in the aura, indicating that faster vibrations of light are passing through the chakras. This "feeds" the chakras, enabling the person's full potential to manifest itself.

THE LOTUS BLOSSOM

Chakras are traditionally symbolically depicted as lotus blossoms. There are similarities between a lotus and a human. It has roots that lie in muddy water (human failings). As it grows it sends a long shoot through the water (our emotions), until the bud reaches the surface and opens to the Sun, displaying a beautiful golden heart (human potential).

Chakras can be described as open or closed "flowers" positioned along the *Sushumna nadi* (spine). From base to crown, each is associated with a number of petals on the lotus blossom. Every set of petals is the color associated with that particular chakra and represents the flow of prana through the nadis and the degree of spiritual practice required to balance the chakra.

The following pages include meditations for each of the seven major chakras, to work through sequentially.

Beauty is not in the face
Beauty is a light in the heart

KAHLIL GIBRAN—*THE EYE OF THE PROPHET*

The first chakra: the base chakra

The base, or root, chakra is the foundation of life. It is positioned at the very bottom of the spine. This chakra initiates life through procreation and represents our will to live. The base chakra draws Earth energy upward through the feet and legs to process and stabilize it. It channels the energy on up the spine in a form the body can handle: as endocrine signals that balance the release of hormones. Unfortunately, we often fail to get the full flow of Earth energy. We become out of touch with nature when we live in cities, always walking on sidewalks with our feet wrapped in shoes and socks made from artificial materials, going to the supermarket for food instead of growing our own and having a relationship with the soil. This modern way of living often results in tiredness and then anemia.

Have you noticed that even in the most polluted, built-up cities, a few large trees manage to survive? They have developed a strong root structure to feed them, which is as large in its spread as the branches above ground. Our "roots" are energy connections, and these need to be strong. This is why awareness of the base chakra will enhance vitality and creativity. Red light, which is the lowest frequency energy of visible light, stimulates this chakra.

RIGHT: *This red, rocky desert landscape is full of the earth energy qualities associated with the base chakra.*

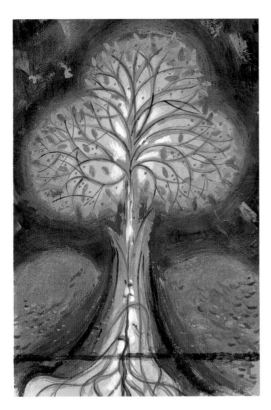

ABOVE: *The Tree of Life, also known as the Tree of Knowledge, is a symbol for human growth in many cultures.*

BASE CHAKRA IMBALANCES

Disorders that affect the sacrum, spine, excretion, and sexual organs are all connected to imbalances of the first chakra. A truly holistic health practice will look for the underlying causes of disease, rather than simply treating the symptoms.

Holistic therapies frequently make a body/mind connection with the subtle energies of the chakras. For example, chronic constipation could be referred to as a base chakra dysfunction caused by holding on to old thoughts and resentments unnecessarily. Diarrhea may also be a base chakra dysfunction, but this may reflect a habit of getting rid of things—rejecting ideas without assimilating them due to deep fear.

Kundalini is curled up at the base of the chakra, like a sleeping snake. This is a metaphor for the powerful, strong, pranic-type life-force that typifies the creative surge of sexual energy that can rise unchecked through the spine and chakras. Spontaneous and sudden awakening of Kundalini will cause pain, heat, loss of control, and other frightening sensations, so esoteric practices such as yoga encourage slow movement of this powerful energy upward through the chakras. But Kundalini is also an energy that the body needs constantly, to revitalize natural cycles of cellular growth and decay—if it is limited, every part of the body will be compromised and experience a lack of life-force. Balancing the chakras assists this revitalization.

During lovemaking, maintaining an upward flow of Kundalini through the chakras and subtle bodies of the aura produces ecstatic responses. This can be learned through Tantric practices, including specialized meditation—but is outside the scope of this book. When we are unable to accept fully our own sexuality, base chakra flow becomes repressed and diseases of the sexual organs can result.

BELOW: *In the Hindu Tantric tradition, erotic carvings symbolize a path to union with the divine.*

Base chakra

Indian name: *Muladhara*

Associated element: *Earth*

Symbol: *Four-petaled lotus flower*

Color of petals: *Vermilion red*

Indian god and goddess: *Brahma and Dakini*

Indian animal: *Elephant with seven trunks*

Key issues: *Sexuality, lust, and obsessions*

Energy function: *Stabilization of Earth energy that enters the body through the feet and legs*

Physical location: *Between the anus and genitals, opening downward*

Associated spinal area: *Fourth sacral vertebra*

Physiological system: *Reproductive*

Endocrine gland: *Gonads*

Nerve plexus: *Sacral-coccygeal*

Activity: *Generation*

Body sense: *Smell*

Inner aspect: *Grounding spiritual energies*

Life lesson: *Survival and establishing purpose on Earth*

Physical action: *Sexuality*

Mental action: *Stability*

Emotional action: *Sensuality*

Spiritual action: *Security*

Gemstones to activate: *Garnet and ruby*

Gemstones to calm: *Emerald and sapphire*

Crystals to balance: *Carnelian and black tourmaline*

Essential oil: *Patchouli*

Planet: *Mars*

Metal: *Iron*

Native American animal: *Snake*

Color for balance/activation: *Red*

Color to calm: *Pink*

BASE CHAKRA
MEDITATIVE VISUALIZATION

This meditation will connect you to the roots of the collective unconscious mind of humanity, which draws its sustenance from deep in the Earth, like the roots of a tree.

Sit in an upright chair, or in a cross-legged yoga posture, if that is comfortable. You may like to refer to Relaxation Exercise No. 1 on page 21 to ensure full relaxation before you start. Take care to be somewhere you will not be disturbed for approximately half an hour—it could be indoors, but it would be even better outside with your back against a large tree. Wherever you are sitting, your spine must be as straight as possible, with your chin pulled in to straighten the back of your neck.

Look at the picture of the tree opposite. Then close your eyes, and breathe slowly and deeply for a few minutes.

Be aware of the ground beneath you (even if you are in a building on a floor above ground level), and start to visualize a strong root, like a tree root, growing from the very

ABOVE: *Imagine that your body is the trunk of a living tree, supplying you with energy for your spiritual growth.*

bottom of your spine and reaching down into the Earth. Imagine you are a seed that is growing into a tree.

Tiny rootlets are developing from the spinal root that anchors you to the ground. See roots growing from the soles of your feet, seeking out flows of water in the Earth. Even if the wind blows extremely hard you will remain firm, because these roots are very flexible.

Now move from the roots to the trunk. Like the main part of your body, it is a channel through which nourishment from the Earth can flow. Check that your body is finely balanced on either side of the spine. Think about your branches. Are they supple and balanced?

Now, be conscious of your neck and head, and imagine perfectly shaped branches going out in four directions: to north, south, east, and west. Observe the kind of leaves you have

on your tree. Maybe there are flowers or fruit. Maybe the branches are bare. Whatever you see, accept it.

Focus on the inner strength that you have, like a tree, constantly directed up into you from the Earth. Thank the water and the Sun for nourishment, and the wind for the way it removes dead leaves and dead wood. Remember that you are connected to all other trees and all other life on this sacred Earth. Really, nothing is separate: all is one.

When you are ready to finish, start to breathe more deeply. Reach down to your feet and rub them, then rub your legs.

Finally, stand up and stretch your body "as tall as a tree."

You may like to keep a special diary or notebook to record this meditation and make a drawing of "your" tree.

ABOVE: *The leaves of a tree are nourished by the energy traveling from its roots. Channeling this life-giving energy bears spiritual fruit.*

The second chakra: the sacral chakra

The second major chakra is the sacral chakra (sometimes known as the spleen or navel center). It is concerned with assimilation, both of food as well as ideas, which brings about a natural sense of joy. This chakra is where sexuality is transmuted into the creative arts through self-expression.

SYMBOLISM OF THE WATER ELEMENT AND THE MOON

The element of Water is associated with the sacral chakra. In the body, the genitourinary system, including the kidneys, connects with

RIGHT: *Like a tide influenced by the phases of the Moon, our life-force ebbs and flows with cosmic energy.*

this chakra. We need water to begin digestive processes and carry the energy derived from food to our cells. Water then disperses unwanted by-products through the kidneys. The sense of taste is linked to this chakra.

It is well known that the Moon influences the flow of all liquids on the Earth, and in us! When the sacral chakra is fully functioning, the water taken into our bodies can be encoded with an imprint of cosmic forces transduced through the Moon. This enables us to keep in harmony with the flow of tides, phases of the Moon, and the psychic changes that occur through life experience. The Moon is therefore depicted as the traditional Indian symbol for this chakra, together with a mythical half-alligator half-fish. Shamanic teaching from Native Americans associates all water creatures with the sacral chakra, including dolphins, which are known to be highly evolved and capable of expressing extreme joy.

SACRAL CHAKRA IMBALANCES

If this chakra is underactive, there will be an urge to overindulge in food or sex, causing obesity, food intolerance, chronic skin con-ditions, or possibly impotence or disease. An overactive sacral chakra will lead to confused sexuality, unless it is balanced by the influence of the heart chakra.

Chakra teachings call us to regain sacral (sacred) equilibrium through dance, laughter (a good "belly" laugh!), yoga, breathing exercises, and visualization of orange light. Even eating orange-colored food will help harmonize this important chakra.

It is at the sacral chakra that caring and homemaking qualities are developed, in both men and women. All relationships and family interactions are functions of the sacral chakra. Consequently, many emotions are handled primarily through this chakra, so it is important to be aware of a possible buildup of stress levels here. Various chakras function in pairs, and psychologically the sacral chakra is linked to the throat chakra. Therefore, if the function

LEFT: *Color and movement combine as Indian gypsies dance. Self-expression helps to maintain a healthy balance in the chakras.*

of the throat chakra is repressed, it will have a detrimental effect on the sacral chakra.

A healer will often work upon both of these chakras in order to bring about equilibrium between them. Clairvoyants (people who see chakras and aura colors clearly—not fortune-tellers) say that this chakra usually has an anticlockwise or "feminine" spin for both men and women, but many factors can change this directional flow.

The key word for the sacral chakra is relationships, at all levels.

ANCESTRAL AND KARMIC LINKS

There are many definitions of Karma. In India, it is considered to be the continual wheel of birth, death, and rebirth. Sometimes it is referred to as the law of cause and effect or "as you sow, so shall you reap." Another thought–provoking definition is "Karma is an expression of the degree to which we have become separate from the Creator/God." Karma is closely linked to the sacral chakra because it is said to carry the memories of ancestral and family issues from past lives.

LEFT: *The Buddhist Bhava-chakra, or Wheel of Life, showing a succession of human existences, all influenced by one another.*

41

Sacral chakra

Indian name: *Svadisthana*

Associated element: *Water*

Symbol: *Six-petaled lotus flower*

Color of petals: *Orange-gold*

Indian god and goddess: *Vishnu and Rakini*

Indian animal: *Makara, mythical creature that is half-alligator, half-fish*

Key issues: *Relationships, violence, and addictions*

Energy function: *Transmutes sexual energy*

Physical location: *Upper part of sacrum, below navel*

Associated spinal area: *First lumbar vertebra*

Physiological system: *Genitourinary*

Endocrine glands: *Adrenals*

Nerve plexus: *Sacral*

Activity: *Excretion*

Body sense: *Taste*

Inner aspect: *Feeling*

Life lesson: *The seeking of meaningful relationships with all life-forms*

Physical action: *Reproduction*

Mental action: *Creativity*

Emotional action: *Joy*

Spiritual action: *Enthusiasm*

Gemstone to activate: *Fire opal and carnelian*

Gemstone to calm: *Emerald*

Crystals to balance: *Moonstone and aquamarine*

Essential oil: *Sandalwood*

Planets: *Venus and Mercury*

Metals: *Copper and Mercury*

Native American animal: *Aquatic animals*

Color for balance/activation: *Orange*

Colors to calm: *Peach and amber*

SACRAL CHAKRA MEDITATIVE VISUALIZATION

"Do not judge a man until you have walked a mile in his moccasins."

NATIVE AMERICAN WISDOM

All life on our planet needs water. This meditation connects you to your emotions and the water in your body, sometimes called the sacred liquids of blood, lymph, semen, sweat, and tears.

Find a quiet place where you will not be disturbed. If possible, cleanse your room with the fragrant-smelling smoke of an incense stick. Prepare yourself in the same way as you have done for other meditations by using a relaxation exercise, if necessary (see pages 21 and 23). Light a white candle and place it where it can burn safely. If you possess a moonstone, hold it in your left hand, or put a small bowl of fresh water, with a flower floating in it, nearby. You may sit, or lie down if you are not sleepy.

Look at the bowl of water, then at the picture of the ocean on the opposite page. Close your eyes and breathe slowly and deeply

ABOVE: *Vibrant orange-gold petals, the fruit of a plant's life-energy, form a flower in the color of the sacral chakra.*

for a few minutes. Imagine waves of relaxation washing over your body, releasing any anxieties. Try to establish a wavelike rhythm in your breathing.

See yourself very safely supported on the surface of a calm sea, within sight of the shore. The water is warm, the sunshine pleasant. The gentle swell of the water rocks you back and forth. You become even more relaxed.

Begin to sense that the ocean is balancing all of the fluids in your body, so that they begin to function in harmony.

Gradually the Sun sets and a brilliant orange light fills the western sky.

The scene changes to moonlight. Still floating on the water, you allow the silvery caress of the Moon to harmonize your emotions and relationships with your lover, family, and friends.

When you are ready to finish, slowly allow your senses to become aware of the room that you are in. Breathe a little deeper for a few moments, and stretch.

Drink the water in the flower bowl, then continue the day in an unhurried way. Remember to record your experiences in a meditation diary.

Please note that if you feel very emotional, it is best to do just the basic relaxation and breathing exercises described earlier. Always seek the advice of a trained counselor if you feel you cannot cope alone.

ABOVE: *Waves roll in and out like the breath, sweeping a tide of relaxation and calm through the body.*

The third chakra: the solar plexus chakra

A yogi describes this chakra as a city of jewels, for it is a precious, powerful link to the body. It is here that the element of Fire rules and the Sun's energies, charged with prana, are stored. Here also the upward-flowing Earth energy meets the downward-flowing cosmic energy.

The chakra's action on the body's glandular system is through the pancreas, which produces insulin and is involved in the metabolism of sugar. The physical location of the solar plexus chakra stretches from the bottom of the breastbone (sternum) to the navel, covering a large area that includes the stomach, gall bladder, and liver—organs primarily concerned with the digestive system. The sympathetic nervous system and the health of the muscles are also influenced by it.

BELOW: *Native Americans often use traditional dance rituals to invoke healing energy.*

SOLAR PLEXUS CHAKRA IMBALANCES

This is a vital center to treat during illness. If negative emotions in the sacral chakra are not dealt with, they can rise to the solar plexus chakra and overstimulate it. Overactivity of the solar plexus chakra leads to misuse of personal power, while underactivity leads to introversion. A happily balanced chakra allows personal empowerment that honors the wisdom and knowledge of others.

Two diseases are associated with this chakra—diabetes and cancer. With diabetes, a holistic practitioner may work with a client to establish reasons why he or she does not allow sweetness (both sugar and sweetness of personality) to be properly absorbed. In cancer sufferers this chakra is often found to be

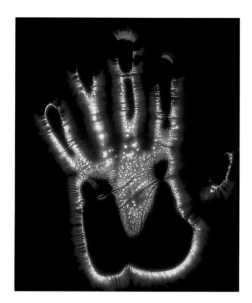

holding on to unprocessed emotions of anger, fear, or hate. Balancing the solar plexus chakra to ensure that it processes energies from the lower chakras as well as the heart chakra may be achieved through healing, meditation, visualization, crystals (particularly emerald or citrine), and by just breathing in the power of the Sun. This should not replace conventional medical treatment, but it does enhance the body's desire to support its own healing.

THE SUN

The Sun transduces (converts) energies from outside our solar system and directs them to the planets. The Sun has often been used as a metaphor for Divinity or God. Native Americans, as well as many other cultures, revere their cosmic connections, naming Father Sun, Mother Earth, and Sister Moon. By honoring the Sun, they strengthen connections to their solar plexus chakra—they find pleasure in simple amusements, are less troubled by stress, and tend to have a fiery nature that releases negative emotions quickly. Prayers and offerings to the Sun are an everyday part of their culture.

KIRLIAN PHOTOGRAPHY

Kirlian photography is a specialist area of research using what is called "the corona discharge" phenomenon (a pattern of electron flow around a grounded object). It makes a fingerprint look like a Sun with streamers of energy coming from it. The differences in the patterns on Kirlian photos can be analyzed to detect imbalances at many levels of the chakras and physical disease.

GUT FEELINGS

Having a "gut feeling" means to sense something at a very deep level. This is the solar plexus chakra in action, part of a process to discriminate between good and bad feelings or emotions. Maybe you have felt "butterflies in your stomach," or a tightening of the whole area just before an important event happens. This is the chakra closing down a little and pulling in and slightly away from the physical body as a form of protection.

The seat of the emotions lies within this chakra. Our emotions are processed through the solar plexus chakra, where fire energy burns them up. Like a real fire, the ashes of the burned emotions need to be raked out every so often in order for the fire to continue to burn strongly. The ideal is to rise above a constant buffeting by negative emotions—not to become emotionless or uncaring—but to register, understand, and then release them. In this way the chakra stays in constant equilibrium and is able to resist emotional stress.

AFFIRMATION
I honor the power of life-giving Sun.

Solar plexus chakra

Indian name: *Manipura*

Associated element: *Fire*

Symbol: *Ten-petaled lotus flower*

Color of petals: *Yellow-gold*

Indian god and goddess: *Rudra and Lakini*

Indian animal: *Ram (male sheep)*

Key issues: *Power, fear, anxiety, and introversion*

Energy function: *Transduces solar and pranic energy*

Physical location: *Between navel and bottom of sternum*

Associated spinal area: *7th and 8th thoracic vertebrae*

Physiological system: *Metabolic/digestive*

Endocrine gland: *Islets of Langerhans (groups of cells in the pancreas)*

Nerve plexus: *Solar plexus*

Activity: *Movement*

Body sense: *Sight*

Inner aspect: *Opinion and personal power*

Life lesson: *Honoring wisdom of others, leading to personal empowerment*

Physical action: *Digestion*

Mental action: *Power*

Emotional action: *Expansiveness*

Spiritual action: *Growth*

Gemstone to activate: *Topaz*

Gemstones to calm: *Emerald and sapphire*

Crystal to balance: *Citrine*

Essential oil: *Sage*

Planets: *Sun and Moon*

Metals: *Gold and silver*

Native American animal: *Birds*

Color for balance/activation: *Golden yellow*

Color to calm: *Violet*

This meditation connects to your Sun energy within, helping you to achieve a fiery vitality.

Ensure that you will not be disturbed. Ideally, clear your room of static energies that can encumber the aura by lighting a sage stick (a bundle of herbs known as a "smudge stick," which is available in many New Age stores) and allowing it to smolder gently. Go all around the room with the stick (this is called "smudging"), so the smoke drifts into all the corners. You may also use a specially chosen feather, of any color you wish, to waft the sweet-smelling smoke into areas of stagnation. Have a fireproof bowl of sand or earth ready to extinguish the sage stick. If you are unable to do smudging, put three drops of sage essential oil in the water of an oil vaporizer (burner). Experiment with these methods—you may find that the smoke tends to induce sleep, but the essential oil wakes you up.

Light a candle. Go through one of the relaxation exercises on pages 21 or 23 if you

ABOVE: *Moving a smudge stick around the body purifies the aura by encouraging static energy to begin flowing again.*

wish, then sit and relax, looking at the picture on this page. Close your eyes.

Breathe slowly and deeply, and with each breath become more aware of the solar plexus chakra at the front of your body.

As you breathe in, imagine a brilliant golden yellow Sun at the chakra. Feel its warmth and vitality.

As you breathe out, imagine the warming energy spreading down to your feet and up to your head. Continue breathing in this way, allowing any distressing or negative emotions to flow away from you, until you feel that the chakra is balanced.

Now that you are working more deeply with chakras, it is vital to ask verbally for the chakra to close down to an appropriate level when the meditation finishes, so that you will feel ready for the outside world. At the same time, you should visualize the chakra closing down. Protect the chakra by visualizing a golden circle with a flaming Sun at the center, over the solar plexus. Finally, slowly open your eyes and blow out the candle flame.

ABOVE: *Sunflower petals vibrate with energy-giving color, flooding the solar plexus with light.*

The fourth chakra: the heart chakra

The heart chakra is positioned in the center of the chest and is connected to two other minor chakras, the thymus (a newly developing chakra) and the kalpatree. The associated colors of lights to balance them are, respectively, bright grass-green and pinkish violet or gold. The Sanskrit word for the heart, *anahata*, means "unstruck"—the place where sound or the source of creation manifests itself. The heart chakra is regarded as a gateway to higher consciousness.

Our hands are included in the flow of heart chakra energies, and it is through them that we can experience the gift of touch. When a group of us sit or stand in a circle holding hands, we move a constant wave of energy around the circle—it goes from the left hand, across the chest, and out of the right hand.

TOUCH EXERCISE
Try this on your own or with a friend. Your left hand should be more receptive to receiving energy, the right hand to giving. Sit down and close your eyes. Gently, with a featherlike movement, touch your left hand (or your friend's left hand) with the tips of your right fingers, and notice what it feels like. Now stroke the left hand firmly, moving from wrist to fingers. Next, use your right thumb to press all over the left palm—notice which kind of touch you (or your friend) like best. Afterward, shake your hands toward the ground to release any unwanted energies, then, if you are practicing with a friend, change over.

THE ROSE OF LOVE
The heart is the place where unconditional love and compassion develop. These can be encouraged by first balancing the heart chakra with the color green, and then bringing in a soft pink. If using crystals for this type of healing, hold a cleansed green aventurine to the heart chakra, followed by a rose quartz. Sometimes the chakra is visualized as a beautiful rose—red for energy, pink for love, or white for purity. This visualization may allow deep issues to surface—so beware, the rose has thorns!

HEART CHAKRA IMBALANCES
The circulation of air and oxygenated blood through the body are functions of this chakra. Energy blockages in the heart chakra may manifest themselves as heart or lung disease. The flow of lymph may also be affected. When the heart chakra and its two associated minor

RIGHT: *Energy from the heart flows toward other people along the arm and through the thumb and fingertips.*

ABOVE: *Areas of pink in the aura are manifestations of an emotional state of unconditional love and compassion.*

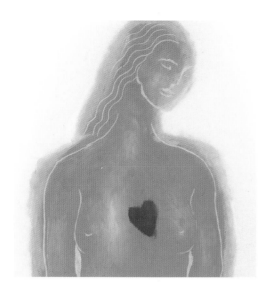

ABOVE: *The heart is the center of the body's circulatory system, which carries oxygen and nutrition to the tissues.*

chakras begins—the development of forgiveness, peace, acceptance, openness, harmony, and contentment, all of which are aspects of unconditional divine love.

TAKING NATURE TO HEART

In our Western culture we have become quite separate from the world of nature, seeing it as something "out there" to be enjoyed on weekends. Yet we too are part of this world, and our every thought and action has an effect upon it. This occurs mainly through our heart chakra. When actively working to develop this chakra for positive personal growth, we automatically resonate more with nature.

There is much to learn from peoples who still live simply, with few material goods. They often shine with an inner spirit and brilliance rarely seen among the inhabitants of busy modern cities, because their whole way of living has intensified the flow of energies through their chakras. We too can achieve this zest for life, but first we need to apply ourselves to creating the conditions in which to find such simplicity.

chakras (the thymus and the kalpatree) are fully balanced, the physical body automatically enters a state where its basic survival needs are met. It is then that the real work of these

AFFIRMATION

Creation is a precious jewel in the lotus of my heart.

LEFT: *The Native American way of life, characterized by simplicity, has allowed its people space for spiritual development.*

Heart chakra

Indian name: *Anahata*

Associated element: *Air*

Symbol: *Twelve-petaled lotus flower*

Color of petals: *Grass green*

Indian god and goddess: *Isha and Kakini*

Indian animal: *Antelope*

Key issues: *Passion, tenderness, inner child issues, and rejection*

Energy function: *Receptor/distributor of unconditional love energy*

Physical location: *Center of chest on sternum*

Associated spinal area: *Fourth thoracic vertebra*

Physiological systems: *Circulatory, lymphatic, and immune systems*

Endocrine gland: *Thymus*

Nerve plexus: *Heart plexus*

Activity: *Manipulation*

Body sense: *Touch*

Inner aspect: *Unconditional love and compassion*

Life lesson: *Honoring the earthly forms of divine love*

Physical action: *Circulation*

Mental action: *Passion*

Emotional action: *Love*

Spiritual action: *Devotion*

Gemstone to activate: *Emerald*

Gemstones to calm: *Sapphire and topaz*

Crystals to balance: *Aventurine, rose quartz, rhodonite, and rhodocrosite*

Essential oil: *Rose*

Planets: *Venus and Mercury*

Metals: *Copper and Mercury*

Native American animal: *Mammals*

Color for balance/activation: *Spring green*

Colors to calm: *Magenta and pink*

HEART CHAKRA MEDITATIVE VISUALIZATION

"May my heart be in the heart of the Universe.
May the heart of the Universe be in my heart.
May my heart be in the heart of the Earth,
May the heart of the Earth be in my heart."

PRAYER FROM THE INDIGENOUS MAYA
ELDERS OF CENTRAL AMERICA

This is a meditation to link you to Earth and sky through the element of Air. If possible, use rose essential oil in an oil vaporizer, have a rose in a vase in the room, or hold a rose quartz crystal during the meditation.

Ensure that you will not be disturbed. Light a candle. Sit and relax, looking at the picture opposite, then close your eyes. Remember to keep your spine straight.

ABOVE: *Holding rose quartz balances the heart chakra as your breath links your energies to the elemental force of Air.*

Breathe slowly and deeply, feeling the expansion of your lungs. Listen to your heartbeat. Notice the expansion of your chest as you breathe. Breathe in all aspects of the nature element of Air, ranging from stormy winds to gentle breezes.

Visualize the heart chakra as a beautiful rose. Concentrate on observing its color and whether the flower is a tightly shut bud or fully open bloom.

Find the place where the rose is growing—you can see the whole bush, the sky, earth, and leaves. Focus on your own rose, a single bloom, again. Notice if it has changed and if its center of golden stamens is visible.

When you are ready to finish, ask the rose to close its petals, then put a circle of bright green light around it, asking for the protection of your own heart chakra.

Finally, put your right hand crossways across your chest, followed by the left in the same manner. Open your eyes and blow out the candle.

As with all chakra meditative visualizations, it is a good idea to record your experiences in a diary, and make a drawing of your rose.

ABOVE: *Air moves across the surface of the Earth in a gentle breeze. The flower of your heart chakra is part of the living color of nature.*

The fifth chakra: the throat chakra

Try to think of the throat chakra as a bridge, because it is placed at a physical point on the neck where the body narrows and concentrates all of its energies to pass information up to the brain.

It is a bridge too in the sequential development of the inner aspects of chakra energies, since once the throat chakra is open, access to a different land, another side of the "river of life"—the spiritual realms—is achievable. This chakra's associated nature element is Ether, a nebulous energy, mysteriously supporting other dimensions of soul and spirit.

In the yoga symbol for the throat chakra, the lotus petals are sometimes smoky blue, representing the Ether. The symbolic animal, an elephant without a yoke, indicates the

inherent strength and power that can be developed from this chakra.

The throat chakra is linked primarily to the thyroid and parathyroid glands in the body. These glands secrete hormones for normal human growth and metabolism of calcium. The workings of the ear, nose, and throat, with the senses of hearing and speech, and to some extent the respiratory system, are also connected to this chakra. So if there are imbalances in any of these areas, which will show up as disease or discomfort, the throat chakra will need to receive healing.

HELPING OFFENDERS

The power of chakras is even being used to help offenders in society: for example, some European prisons now teach yoga and meditation to inmates. In one jail for young offenders in Britain, Reiki healing (see page 123) has been used effectively with teenage drug abusers. From these examples it is also possible to see a developed awareness of the power of self-expression (the main quality of the throat chakra) on the part of the teachers, and their ability to share it with others (the province of the heart chakra). Clairvoyants report that drug or alcohol abuse can cause chakras to be open for too long or to fluctuate wildly in their action, causing great confusion (the chakras should open and close naturally). The body will sense that these substances are pollutants and attempt to get rid of them, which will put additional strain on all the chakras.

THROAT CHAKRA BLOCKAGES

If this chakra is blocked, it can result in depression and may even make a person feel suicidal. If you are very depressed, it may help

RIGHT: *Nelson Mandela, the South African statesman who spoke out against apartheid, has a strong sense of personal strength.*

SPEAKING OUR TRUTH

"Our deepest fear is not that we are inadequate. Our deepest fear is that we are powerful beyond measure. It is our light, not our darkness, that most frightens us. We ask ourselves, who am I to be brilliant, gorgeous, talented, and fabulous? Actually, who are you not to be? You are a child of God. Your playing small doesn't serve the world..."

NELSON MANDELA, INAUGURAL SPEECH, 1994

to discuss your problems with a qualified counselor. By talking things through, you will encourage the self-expression aspect of the throat chakra.

There are also other ways of combating depression. For example, it is possible to use the color turquoise-blue, associated with this chakra, which may be given by a color practitioner or healer as colored light. Professional treatment can be backed up by obtaining a turquoise crystal or by regular visualization of this color. There is more about this in the chapters on color and crystals. You could also try the simple remedy of wearing a turquoise silk scarf around your neck.

BELOW: *Good use of color is second nature in many cultures. This Moroccan stallholder's scarf keeps his throat chakra balanced.*

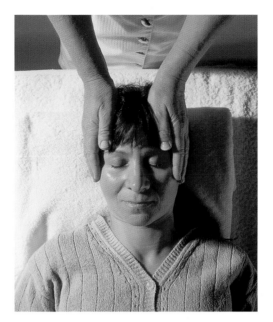

LEFT: *A Reiki therapist sends energy through her hands into the patient to clear a blockage.*

AFFIRMATION
I will express my higher wisdom to others.

Throat chakra

Indian name: *Vishuddha*

Associated element: *Ether (Akasha)*

Symbol: *Six-petaled lotus flower*

Color of petals: *Turquoise or smoky blue*

Indian god and goddess: *Sadasiva and Sakini*

Indian animal: *Elephant*

Key issues: *Self-expression, communication, and will*

Energy function: *Acts a a bridge between physical and spiritual energies*

Physical location: *Between collarbone and larynx on the neck*

Associated spinal area: *Third cervical vertebra*

Physiological system: *Respiratory*

Endocrine glands: *Thyroid/parathyroid*

Nerve plexus: *Cervical ganglia*

Activity: *Speech*

Body sense: *Hearing*

Inner aspect: *Expression*

Life lesson: *To resonate with compassion*

Physical action: *Communication*

Mental action: *Fluent thought*

Emotional action: *Independence*

Spiritual action: *Inspiration*

Gemstone to activate: *Topaz*

Gemstones to calm: *Sapphire and emerald*

Crystals to balance: *Turquoise and gem silica*

Essential oil: *Lavender*

Planets: *Mars and Jupiter*

Metals: *Iron and tin*

Native American animal: *Humans*

Color for balance/activation: *Turquoise*

Color to calm: *Pale misty blue*

THROAT CHAKRA MEDITATIVE VISUALIZATION

This meditation will strengthen your immune system, increase your energy levels, and combat any feelings of depression. Note that there are usually many stages of recovery between feeling ill and regaining full health. It is at these times of convalescence that visualization using the color turquoise can be particularly helpful.

Spend around three minutes looking at the picture of the blue flower opposite, absorbing the rich color of its petals.

When you are ready, lie down in the yoga relaxation position described on page 21. If you are feeling sleepy, sit up. Play some gentle music if you find it helpful. Go through the relaxation procedure (see page 21). Your body needs to be deeply relaxed for deep healing to take place.

Now think of anything that you would like to change in your body. Think of any aches or pains you have. Strongly visualize gathering them all together into a ball, and see it turn into a dark-blue balloon.

ABOVE: *Visualize your discomforts as a dark cloud of air, and imagine the cloud of air filling a balloon. You hold the string attached to the balloon. Let go of the string, and watch your problems float away and dissolve as the balloon bursts.*

Let the balloon float slowly upward into a clear, pale-blue sky. As it rises almost out of sight, it bursts, and changes into a flower with beautiful turquoise petals. Repeat this balloon and flower visualization time and time again, until you feel that you have got rid of all of your worries and problems.

When you are ready to finish, concentrate on your incoming breath. See it as an orange glow of energy that recharges your body completely and adjusts all the chakras into a beautiful balance.

Sit up slowly. Record your experiences in a diary if you wish.

ABOVE: *The vibrant blue of the Himalayan poppy disperses gloom and encourages the body's ability to heal itself.*

The sixth chakra: the brow chakra

This chakra, situated at the center of the brow, represents the inner eye and is sometimes called the third eye or eye of wisdom.

The yogic symbol for the brow chakra depicts a lotus with two petals, but actually they are two sides (like the two hemispheres of the brain), each of 48 petals. These two sides represent everything that has a dual aspect, such as light and dark, female and male, hot and cold, and the duality and battle that occurs between ego and spirit in this chakra. All too often, our ego thinks it supplies us with everything we need, and the chakra remains undeveloped and almost shut down. The ideal is to balance this center so that the chakra is fully open to its enormous potential and so that spirit can also manifest itself. Sometimes the ego is known as our lower self and spirit as our higher self.

RIGHT: *Children find it easy to detect auras. This ability is not usually encouraged and is lost as we grow older.*

AFFIRMATION

I manifest my Karmic inheritance—now.

ESP

Extrasensory perception (ESP) is the ability to use intuitive abilities, which originates at the brow chakra, assisted by two minor chakras at the temples. The ability to see beyond the physical world is called clairvoyance—clear seeing. Hearing sounds or voices not in the physical world is called clairaudience—clear hearing. Sensing smells and perfumes not of this world is called clairsentience.

Some people appear to be born with such abilities and if these qualities are recognized and allowed to develop, they often work as clairvoyants, mediums, or healers. Children frequently perceive auras around people, believing it is the natural way to see things—and of course it is—but unthinking adults will take them to have their eyes tested! Nowadays more babies are being born to enlightened parents who recognize the importance of encouraging these abilities. In general, there is an upsurge of interest in mysticism and spirituality. Just to see the range of books available on these subjects, compared to 25 years ago, shows the funda-mental change that is taking place in human consciousness.

THE BODY'S COMMAND CENTER

The brow and crown chakras specialize in transmuting the energies of a multidimensional universe. They are linked to the control system of endocrine glands that affects the physiology of the body from cellular gene to the function-ing of the central nervous system.

The pituitary gland is associated with the brow chakra. Its secretions provide a deep connection between the brain and the immune system, hinting at how emotional trauma experienced and recorded through the brain can create physical illness.

Finally, the pineal gland, which is receptive to light, becomes active when the crown chakra is open. With its links to the pituitary, it enhances psychic levels, allowing a person to "see within," or to have "second sight."

LEFT: *A church door in Greece is protected by an apotropaic eye—a symbolic eye believed to ward off evil. The eye prevents dangerous spirits from entering the sacred building by reflecting their dark qualities back toward them.*

THIRD EYE IMBALANCES

Do you have frequent headaches, particularly migraines, or sinus or ear problems, or endocrine imbalances? At an energy level, these problems can be caused by not wanting to see or hear something that is vitally important to the growth of the soul. Follow the proverb that says—"Do not put off until tomorrow something that can be done today." Working with visualization exercises, particularly those concentrating on the third eye, will help to combat these problems and encourage physical and spiritual well-being.

BELOW: *Some reptiles have a pineal gland linked to a light-sensitive area or rudimentary third eye, with a lens and retina-type photoreceptor cells. It is thought this enables them to see ranges of light, such as infrared, and ultraviolet, that are invisible to the human eye.*

Brow chakra

Indian name: *Ajna*

Associated element: *Spirit*

Symbol: *Two-petaled lotus flower*

Color of petals: *Deep indigo blue*

Indian god and goddess: *Shiva and Shakti Hakini*

Indian animal: *None*

Key issues: *Balancing higher and lower selves, and trusting inner guidance*

Energy function: *Merging masculine and feminine energies*

Physical location: *Center of the brow*

Associated spinal area: *First cervical vertebra*

Physiological systems: *Endocrine and nervous systems*

Endocrine gland: *Pituitary*

Nerve plexus: *Hypothalamus and pituitary*

Activity: *Insight*

Body sense: *Clairvoyance*

Inner aspect: *Intuition*

Life lesson: *Completing Karmic lesson of this lifetime*

Physical action: *Visualization*

Mental action: *Intuition*

Emotional action: *Clarity*

Spiritual action: *Meditation*

Gemstone to activate: *Diamond*

Gemstones to calm: *Sapphire and emerald*

Crystal to balance: *Lapiz lazuli*

Essential oil: *Frankincense*

Planets: *Uranus and Saturn*

Metals: *Silver and lead*

Native American animal: *All spirit guides, ancestors, and multidimensional beings of light*

Color for balance/activation: *Ultramarine*

Color to calm: *Indigo blue*

BROW CHAKRA
MEDITATIVE VISUALIZATION

This yogic technique is called *Tratakam*, and should be performed sitting in a dark room in front of a candle placed around 3ft (1m) away, preferably at eye level. If you have epilepsy you may prefer not to do this visualization with a candle—if this is the case, just go deeply into the image on the photograph opposite. Look at the photograph and sense the amazing and unfathomable harmony of space.

First ensure that you are sitting comfortably, with a straight spine, your legs uncrossed if you are sitting on a chair, or adopt a yoga sitting posture if you are on the floor. Close your eyes and take three slow, deep breaths.

Open your eyes and look straight at the candle flame. Without straining your eyes, keep them focused on the flame. You can blink when you feel it is necessary. When your eyes do begin to get tired, close them.

With your eyelids closed, look upward to the position of your brow chakra. See an

ABOVE: *The flickering candle flame helps to focus the mind. Let go of any distracting thoughts and allow your mind to concentrate only on the flame. When you close your eyes, its image will appear clearly near your brow chakra.*

image there of the candle flame, and many colors. The colors may appear different from normal. They may move around and then disappear. When they do, endeavor to bring the image of the flame back. Try to hold the inner image for as long as possible.

When the image of the flame has finally disappeared, keep your eyes closed and pause. You may see more inner light and vibrant color. If you do, just watch—don't judge or try to guess what it might be. If something wants

to reveal itself to you in the form of a picture— then it will.

After no longer than 30 minutes, open your eyes, rub the palms of your hands together vigorously, then gently place your palms over both eyes to rest them.

When you have finished, it can be helpful to make a record of anything about the meditation in your diary. You may also find it useful to draw pictures to help you remember the experience in more detail.

ABOVE: *The infinity and depth of space symbolizes the universal energy and allows the essence of the mind to be free.*

The seventh chakra: the crown chakra

The crown or thousand-petaled lotus is the chakra that activates and opens us up to higher consciousness. The two basic energies of duality, which we name masculine and feminine, unite, bond, and transcend at this chakra, creating (when it is fully active) a super-consciousness that is beyond time and space. In this super-consciousness, a process of unification occurs between the human personality and a Higher Self. Tiny jewels of "all that is, all that has been, and all that ever will be" are carried as soul seeds from one lifetime to another.

When we begin to have even a small glimpse of what these words mean, it is like an enormous power being lit up in the mind. People have described this experience in many different ways: "the top of my head felt as if it was splitting," "a fountain of divine light flowed in and out," and "I was taken into the light." Once we begin to have these kind of experiences, there is no going back. Mundane, everyday life is forever changed, and we see everything as a play of subtle energies, sometimes identified with the rainbow of liberated energy of Tantric Buddhism.

CROWN CHAKRA BALANCE

Influencing the head, this chakra opens upward. It connects deep within the brain to the pineal gland, which is an important key to our biological clock.

The pineal gland and the gonads (prostate/testes or ovaries/uterus at the base chakra) work closely together to regulate sexual growth at puberty. The pineal gland produces a hormone called melatonin, which regulates the light-reactive photoreceptors in the retina of the eye. Continuous light decreases melatonin production, and increased production in the dark at night calms us down. In women, during the 28-day menstrual cycle, peaks occur in melatonin production, stimulated by light levels and particular wavelengths of light. During the day, the pineal gland produces high levels of another hormone, serotonin, urging us into activity. So these two hormones work in a continuous circadian cycle. Serotonin is thought to have an important influence on our emotional state—high levels of the hormone are thought to improve mood.

Various other hormones released by the pineal gland, including pinoline, are similar to LSD, producing hallucinations and heightened states of awareness. The pineal gland also has a complex biological link with the adrenal glands, which produce adrenaline, the "flight or fight" hormone. This link is thought to influence stress levels, through the kidneys and guts, at the solar plexus and sacral chakras.

CONCLUSION

We have seen that through the pineal gland the crown chakra is biologically linked to the whole endocrine system and the rhythm of waking and sleeping. Seasonal Affective

RIGHT: *In Hinduism, the gods and goddesses represent Brahman, the supreme spirit.*

AFFIRMATION

I manifest the pure Light of Spirit.

ABOVE: *When an animal enters the deep sleep of hibernation, its body temperature drops and its physiological processes slow down, returning to normal when it wakes in the spring.*

Disorder (SAD) is a type of depression reflecting unnatural cycles of sleep (natural rhythms would be to sleep at dusk and waken at dawn). It is caused by an imbalance of the melatonin/serotonin cycle as a result of the artificiality of street lighting, sleeping with drapes closed, night work, and so on, and can be improved by using a special light, which mimics natural daylight, in the winter.

Medical research continues to throw more "light" upon pineal functions, at the same time reinforcing chakra wisdom teachings. For example, melatonin production reaches its peak at around 3 a.m., according to biologists, so the crown chakra is therefore most receptive to meditation at this time.

LEFT: *The excess of artificial light in the Western world can interrupt the body's natural sleeping patterns.*

The pineal gland of some hibernating animals causes them to sleep throughout the winter in response to reduced daylight.

Crown chakra

Indian name: *Sahasrara*

Associated element: *Spirit*

Symbol: *Thousand-petaled lotus*

Color of petals: *White, violet, or gold*

Indian god and goddess: *Shiva and Shakti*

Indian animal: *None—represents enlightened human*

Key issues: *Inner wisdom and aging.*

Energy function: *Unity and transcending masculine and feminine energy*

Physical location: *Top of head*

Associated spinal area: *None*

Physiological system: *Central nervous system and brain.*

Endocrine gland: *Pineal*

Nerve plexus: *Cerebral cortex*

Activity: *Transcendence*

Body sense: *ESP—clairvoyance, clairsentience, and clairaudience*

Inner aspect: *Release*

Life lesson: *Releasing attachments in order to transcend earthbound Karma*

Physical action: *Meditation*

Mental action: *Universal consciousness*

Emotional action: *Beingness*

Spiritual action: *Unity*

Gemstone to activate: *Sapphire*

Gemstone to calm: *Emerald*

Crystals to balance: *Clear quartz and amethyst*

Essential oil: *Ylang-ylang*

Planet: *Neptune*

Metal: *Platinum*

Native American animal: *Kachina, symbol of Universal Spirit embodied in all animate life.*

Color for balance/activation: *Golden-white light*

Color to calm: *Pale rose-pink*

CROWN CHAKRA MEDITATIVE VISUALIZATION

This meditation is best performed outside in a quiet spot, if possible. However, if you prefer to stay inside, you should prepare your room by lighting a candle, adding 3 drops of ylang-ylang essential oil to the water of an oil vaporizer (burner), and placing some fresh flowers in front of you, if possible. It may also help to hold a clear quartz crystal in your left hand.

1 Sit in an upright chair, keeping your spine straight and your legs uncrossed, or, if you prefer to sit on the floor, try to adopt a cross-legged yoga sitting posture. Look at the picture of the mountaintop opposite—you can use it as a symbol to represent your highest ideals and aspirations.

2 Relax your body and breathe slowly and deeply. If you find it difficult to relax, you

ABOVE: *Let your mind transport you into a mountainous landscape. The highest mountain is a symbol of your spiritual aspirations. Travel to its summit in your mind. Here, you will discover the power of your crown chakra.*

might find it helpful to go through the relaxation exercise on page 21 first.

3 Focus on your base chakra, sensing the energies there and allowing them to balance.

4 Now focus on each chakra in turn, sensing the energies and allowing them to balance: base chakra, sacral chakra, solar plexus chakra, heart chakra, throat chakra, brow chakra, crown chakra.

5 Imagine that the crown chakra, just above your head, is a beautiful flower of light with a golden center. Sense how far the flower extends into the aura.

6 The tip of each flower petal has a tiny thread of light running from it up to the source of divine light in the cosmos. Establish a two-way flow between yourself and the cosmos, allowing the petals to be open, and to receive. Draw the light of the cosmos into the golden stamens at the center of the flower and run it down your body to your feet, and then on into the Earth. Affirm that you are re-establishing your link with Creation.

7 When you are ready to finish, close the petals of your crown chakra flower and open your eyes. Record your experiences if you wish, but do not dissipate energy by talking about them to other people.

ABOVE: *Climbing a mountain is a metaphor for your spiritual journey. Sometimes the ground will be rocky, but if you keep your destination in clear sight, you will succeed.*

The rainbow bridge of light and color

Color is all around us. Study a stained-glass church window with sunlight behind it and see the intensity and quality of the light colors coming through. They are very different from pigment colors such as those of paint, printing ink, and clothing. In a similar way, there is a sudden experience of inner color when we begin to meditate, visualizing light and seeing it for the first time with the clear intensity of a rainbow.

Within nature we observe "living color " such as all the different shades of green in a landscape, or incredible shades of red, orange, and peach in a sunset. These colors have profound effects on our chakras, without our even being consciously aware of it. They clear away negative energies and emotions, are drawn into the body when we breathe, bring us joy and contentment, restore out-of-balance chakras, and recharge chakra energies.

Meanings of color

Our seven major chakras resonate at wavelengths of light that we see as color—red, orange, yellow, green, turquoise, blue, and violet. These colors are a blend of many shades, merging from one to another, but each chakra has a basic predominant color. The light wavelengths are measured in nanometers (nm).

RED (780–630NM)
Red is vibrancy, a stimulant giving strength and vitality to the body. It is used therapeutically for energy conditions associated with low blood pressure, inactivity, impotence, and M.E. Red can excite, although too much red may cause anger. Scarlet acts as an aphrodisiac. Dull red in the aura indicates chronic disease or misplaced sexual energy.

ORANGE (630–600NM)
Orange is joyful and stimulates the respiratory and nervous systems, so it is useful as an antidepressant. At the sacral chakra, it can benefit the kidneys and genitourinary system.

YELLOW (600–570NM) AND YELLOW/GREEN (570–550NM)
Yellow is associated with mental processes, detachment, intellect, and critical thought. It is used often therapeutically in the treatment of rheumatism and arthritis for its vibrational links to calcium metabolism. At the solar plexus chakra, it invigorates and increases prana uptake into the physical body. Lemon yellow is used as a laxative, antacid, and expectorant, to expel unwanted matter from the body.

GREEN (550–520NM)
Green is the balancing color, which, as the main expression of nature and vegetation on this planet, plays a critical role in the balance of the Earth body (refer to the Gaia hypothesis outlined on page 98). Therapeutically it is most often used for energy imbalances that need purifying or cleansing where, by balancing the heart chakra, issues concerning self-love can be resolved.

TURQUOISE (520–500NM)
This is the main color used to strengthen the body's immunity against disease. Because it lies between green and deep indigo blue, this color holds the body in a similar natural balance to that between the Earth and the sky.

When it is used at the throat chakra, turquoise calms and strengthens the voice. It is also anti-inflammatory, and helps to reduce tension that is caused by an inability to "speak one's truth."

Daylight electric light bulbs may be purchased and used to give full-spectrum lighting, which is particularly beneficial for reading or artwork, where the higher chakras and centers of perception are involved. Normal light bulbs predominantly give the red end of the spectrum, causing eye and brain to be constantly stimulated, and eventually lead to stress.

RIGHT: *The depth of the colors in this stained glass in Chartres Cathedral changes as the natural light shining through it fluctuates in intensity.*

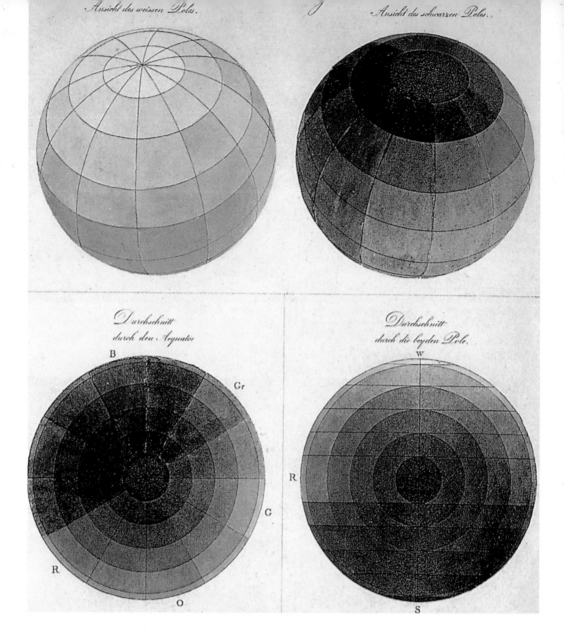

Ansicht des weissen Pols.

Ansicht des schwarzen Pols.

Durchschnitt durch den Aequator.

Durchschnitt durch die beyden Pole.

RIGHT: *This painting by German Romantic painter Philipp Otto Runge (1770–1810) echoes his own mystical color theory that he applied to all his paintings. He assigned the three basic colors to the Divine Trinity: blue/God, red/Son, and yellow/Holy Spirit. The source of the three-dimensional arrangement of the colors on the spheres lay in the main colors being complemented by the two poles of light and darkness to form quintessence of the pure elements.*

BLUE (500—450NM)

Shades of blue in the range between turquoise and indigo are generally very relaxing, and can help to reduce high blood pressure. Just taking a few moments off work to look at the blue of the sky will have this effect. Blue's sedative quality is most often used to balance energy in cases of asthma, migraine, skin irritation, and wounds.

Clear, bright blue is an excellent color for protecting the aura at any time, but especially if you are going into a difficult or challenging situation. On such occasions, you should imagine wrapping a bright blue cloak of light around yourself and all your chakras. The cloak technique is also useful on any occasions where you feel self-protection might be helpful.

VIOLET/PURPLE

(450–380NM) (U.V. 380–320NM)

Violet and purple have a long tradition of spiritual qualities associated with divinity, royalty, and honor. They are used therapeutically to give self-respect—a vital aspect of healing. The spleen and production of white blood corpuscles are stimulated by violet light, and the venous system is stimulated by purple. Both colors lessen sexual desire and are narcotic and hypnotic, particularly when applied to the brow and crown chakras.

Deep personal transformation can be encouraged by the visualization of a sacred violet flame. Eventually, for powerful transmutation, one "steps" into the flame and experiences other spiritual realities.

Other colors

MAGENTA

This color verges on the U.V. (ultraviolet) range. In color therapy it is used to balance green, for it brings expansive and visionary qualities of pure Spirit. Magenta is antiseptic and analgesic. On a scale of vibration it is the next color to ultraviolet, which is used to sterilize surgical instruments.

BLACK

Black is often regarded as a negative color. However, the velvet darkness of space, through which sound and light travel, is quite separate from that of black pigment. Black represents the Earth Goddess, the deep creative "womb" that holds and attracts all colors so that they may be reborn as light.

GRAY

This color indicates authority, control, and repression.

BROWN

The color of earth and wood, which speaks to us as our roots and the basis from which we grow and manifest our "rainbow bridge" of personal auric light and color.

GOLD

This color complements the color brown. Its therapeutic use is for the spine, which can be balanced with gold light visualization or application.

PEACH

Peach is the color red transformed to a higher level of consciousness. According to Steiner (see page 30), it represents the living image of the human soul on Earth. In the event of a death or birth, soft peach-colored light should be used therapeutically, to bathe the surroundings with light, because it eases transition between worlds.

WHITE

White is neutral and is not a color as such. Clear white light actually contains all colors. An absolutely clear white light is often used as a metaphor for Spirit during meditation. Worn as clothing, white indicates purity.

ABOVE: *Gold symbolizes the purity of the universal spirit and is often used in religious art, such as this picture of St. Francis of Assisi.*

Look through a prism and see how images are lit up just like the light of an intensely colored rainbow— or a human aura.

ABOVE: *The eye has color receptors for red, blue, and green. These three colors make up the whole spectrum. Shone onto a white surface, they create white light where they overlap.*

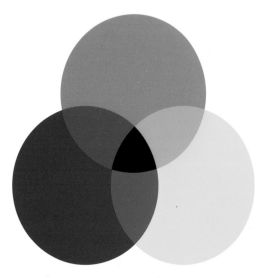

ABOVE: *Color pigment in paint or ink builds up in a completely different way from the colored light of the spectrum, making a darker shade every time a new color is added.*

RIGHT: Strong colors such as red should be used in moderation in the home, to avoid overstimulation.

How to give color to chakras

Color can be added to chakras using crystals, visualization, breathing, light instruments, colored silks, solarized water (see opposite), food, clothes, color bathing, decor, and color acupuncture, all working on subtle energies of aura and chakras. Some methods you can use yourself; others need a color therapist.

COLOR THERAPY

A color therapist will usually treat chakra imbalances by shining colored light through filters or glass. The eye and skin cells absorb particular colors of light and transmit them as vibrations to where they are needed in the body. The body can also absorb color from a cloth placed over particular areas of the skin, in an appropriately lit room. Silk is best for this. A therapist may also use any of the methods described in the paragraph above. They choose colors through experience and a careful assessment of imbalances. Many therapists finish with a complementary (opposite) color to "stop off" the treatment color.

COLOR HEALING

A healer uses his or her hands to scan the body for imbalance, moving them slowly just off the body. When the healer senses that a particular color is needed, he or she may channel it by visualization through the hands to the recipient. This is most effective if the recipient is relaxed. The healer may light a candle and say a prayer before treatment.

Ninety percent of all the information received by our senses comes through the eyes. Twenty-five percent of the body's nutritional intake is required for the functioning of our eyes, even though they make up only two percent of the body's weight. Fifty percent of light information entering the left eye passes to the right hemisphere of the brain, and fifty percent of that entering the right eye passes to the left hemisphere.

RIGHT: Silk, a fine natural fiber, is used by color therapists to transmit color into the body.

COLOR AT WORK AND AT HOME

We all know that computer screens can cause eyestrain. Avoid this by spending five minutes outside every couple of hours. Look at a tree's green leaves, breathe in their color, then place your palms over your eyes for a few seconds. Make sure you have green plants in the office (they also absorb negative electromagnetic fields). Even gazing at green cloth rests the eyes.

The decor in your home can be used to enhance your health. Experiments in growing seeds under different light conditions showed that they do not flourish under green light— we are the same, and green is a color to avoid in paint or indoor lighting. Small areas of red stimulate the first chakra, but large areas are tiring. Orange is a balance between the over-stimulation of red and the detachment of yellow. It is a good color for kitchens or dining rooms. Yellow can be brightening, but too much in a room can cause irrationality or detachment. Combine it with violet or white to lessen these effects. A range of blues can be very calming. If blue seems cold, introduce warm blue/purple tones or orange. Violet is excellent for meditation rooms, churches, and hospitals.

A gray, brown, black, or white room would not help chakra balancing, but white with touches of brilliant color is stimulating, and soft gray with pastel colors is relaxing. Soft peach tones would be suitable for a bedroom and can encourage gentle dreaming. However, too much peach can be unsettling, particularly in an office.

Visualization and meditation

Visualization can lead you to worlds beyond the earthly plane, as well as into deeper meditation. We take ourselves from a fixed time and place, move into other realms, then return to the fixed location. It is as if we need these coordinates as a map reference in order to return to everyday consciousness. Sometimes a fear of losing these coordinates comes up as an inability to focus, shaking, a tugging at the solar plexus chakra, or the body swaying or jolting. Once this is overcome, we can settle into a way of "being" that allows a natural flow of experience through our chakras, both during the visualization practice and in everyday life. The visualization on this page places the beautiful being of light that you are in a rainbow bridge of consciousness between your inner and outer worlds.

WORKING WITH A FRIEND ON COLOR VISUALIZATION

Try these three visualization exercises with a friend, reading them out loud for each other to practice. Obtain a few colored silk cloths.

Exercise 1 Close your eyes and use your intuition to "tune in" to your friend's chakras. You may see a picture, hear words, or just sense which chakras need balancing. Place a cloth on the appropriate part of your partner's body—next to the skin is best, but the color will still reach the skin if he or she is wearing white. Ask your partner to visualize the color and breathe as

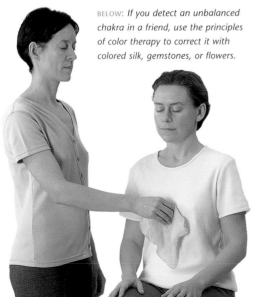

BELOW: *If you detect an unbalanced chakra in a friend, use the principles of color therapy to correct it with colored silk, gemstones, or flowers.*

if drawing in the essence of that color. Not everyone can visualize this immediately—the ability is enhanced by considering the color, not in the abstract, but as a natural object, such as a flower or gem.

Exercise 2 Sit opposite each other with a candle between you. When you are relaxed, send loving energies to each other. This type of energy is unconditional, not sexual. See the energy flow between you in a figure eight movement. This strengthens the movement of your own energy through your chakras and that of your partner.

Exercise 3 Practice the rainbow bridge visualization lying alongside each other, head to feet. A dozen people can all lie head to feet in a star shape, almost touching, to do this.

Lie down and go through the relaxation exercise on page 23. When you are relaxed, start a series of seven deep breaths. Begin at the base chakra and work up, imagining each breath colored in the order of the ascending energy—red, orange, yellow, green, turquoise, indigo, violet. Draw the color into each chakra. Now, breathing naturally, imagine a rainbow arcing over your body. In one breath, breathe in its colors, recharging all the chakras at once. Finally, the rainbow fades but you are held in an intense, clear, golden-white light that fills your body. The light forms a shield that allows only positive energy to pass through. When you are ready, stretch, then curl up your body and sit up slowly.

ABOVE: *Practice your visualization with a friend, and meditate together, opening your heart chakras to send each other unconditional acceptance and love.*

HOW TO MAKE SOLARIZED WATER

Once you have figured out which chakra needs balancing, obtain a small, plain glass jar or bottle in the color of the chakra. Fill the bottle with still spring water and stand it in sunshine for one hour. This charges the water with color energy. Drink the water slowly over an hour or so.

Chakras and sexuality

We all have an individual direction of spin to our chakra energies, clockwise or anticlockwise. Many factors cause the natural spin to reverse temporarily. However, if all seven major chakras are balanced, each one should indicate an alternative motion to the next. Turn to page 115 to find out how to check the spin of a chakra with a pendulum.

Chakras exert an attracting or repelling action, according to their direction. A clockwise chakra attracts an anticlockwise chakra and vice versa. We sometimes become attracted to a sexual partner because of his or her "vibes"—energy messages sent out through the chakras. These relay the direction of spin of the person's chakras, so that during lovemaking a chakra ideally aligns with another of the opposite directional spin. This occurs in both heterosexual and homosexual couples.

By balancing our chakras we will be more likely to attract partners capable of enhancing our auric energy field.

Tantric sex requires training and meditative preparation to liberate chakra energy flow. It moves this enhanced energy upward through the body at climax, and together with the retention of semen, enables lovers to reach

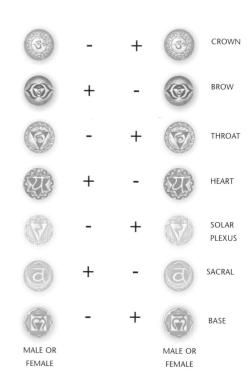

	−	+		CROWN
	+	−		BROW
	−	+		THROAT
	+	−		HEART
	−	+		SOLAR PLEXUS
	+	−		SACRAL
	−	+		BASE
MALE OR FEMALE			MALE OR FEMALE	

a longer-lasting state of bliss. This can only be achieved if both partners have balanced chakras, otherwise the massive surge of sexual release at orgasm will be blocked and will not reach the crown chakra.

PROCREATION

We have already described the action of the chakras during the sacred act of conception. When the experience of blissful sex is working fully through the chakras of the lovers—and it is not just a base chakra experience—the rainbow of bliss becomes an attractive beacon of light for the beautiful soul that is waiting to incarnate. If both partners intend to create a positive new life between them, procreation becomes pro-Creation (for Creation).

THE POWER OF LOVE

Unconditional love presents many challenges. It is about loving ourselves and embarking on the most positive journey of life that is possible, not imposing conditions on another person's love. Central to this relationship with ourselves is our relationship with and love for

the Earth, the "mother" of us all. In the words of the Native American Chief Seattle, spoken in 1854, translated from the Salish language:

"Every part of this Earth is sacred to my people. Every shining pine needle, every sandy shore. Every mist in the dark wood. Every clearing and every humming insect is holy in the memory of my people... If we sell you our land, you must remember and teach your children to give the rivers the kindness that you would give your brother... We are but a strand in the web of life. What we do to the web we do to ourselves. All things are connected."

If we have a good relationship with the planet, we can enjoy fulfilling human relationships, and our chakras will glow with life and the intensity of full experience. If we live in ways that pollute the planet, the fine balance of electromagnetic energies (the same thing as the Native American's web of life) will be damaged and we will not maintain a healthy relationship with our chakras. Unconditional love is given freely, in all areas of our life, without any expectation of personal gain.

ESOTERIC AND EXOTERIC PATTERNS

The web of life on our planet is like a spider's web, holding energy patterns in esoteric (inner) and exoteric (outer) forms. Esoteric patterns are only perceived at subtle levels of other dimensions of understanding, like the spinning chakras most of us cannot actually see, or the flow of auric colors. Exoteric energy patterns are outwardly visible, such as the marks of waves across sand or a tornado. Patterns may combine the esoteric and exoteric; a thin layer of sand on a piece of parchment stretched over a frame responds to sound vibrations made electronically or with a violin bow drawn across its edge, creating patterns as shown below. These illustrations show "interference patterns" in the web of life. A healthily functioning chakra has a particular intrinsic personal pattern. A blocked, imbalanced chakra will have a different, possibly chaotic, pattern. Many of the modalities explored in this book (including color, crystals, pendulums, sound, healing hands, visualization, and color breathing) create an interference overlay of beneficial energy patterns that realigns the energy of chakras that are out of balance.

Laughter "therapy" is now recognized to bring positive health and chakra benefits, because laughing helps to release antistress hormones. Clinical analysis of tears has revealed that tears of laughter have a very different chemical content from tears shed in sorrow.

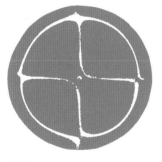

280 C.P.S.

865 C.P.S.

4,500 C.P.S.

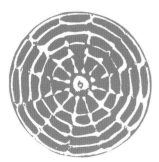

7,500 C.P.S.

9,500 C.P.S.

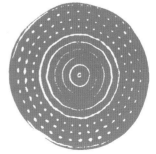

10,000 C.P.S.

LEFT: *1960s German physician, physicist, and musician Dr. Hans Jenny developed the science of cymatics. His photographic images showed effects of sound waves passing through powders and liquids. Sound creates geometric, abstract, and vortical patterns according to cycles per second (cps) frequency and are similar to patterns of chakras seen by mystics.*

The effects of subtle pollution

Our chakras are incredibly sensitive. They respond to many outside stimuli, such as food, environment, and pollution. We subtly sense both pleasurable and painful states through them before the body itself registers an emotion. Whenever we harbor negative emotions, or they are directed at us, our aura takes them in and our chakras react, causing a follow-on effect in the body that eventually wears down our physiological defense systems.

Subtle pollution is less obvious than other types of pollution such as fumes or chemicals. It includes the negative psychological emotions of anger, hatred, and jealousy. Traumatic events, such as an accident or bereavement, or drug abuse, will temporarily or sometimes permanently damage a chakra's response. In some instances the chakras will shut down; in cases of drug or alcohol abuse the chakras will be "wedged open," causing exposure to the pollutant to continue unabated. Such situations are outside the scope of this book, and it would be advisable to consult a qualified healer in these instances.

CHECKING EMFS

The effects of electromagnetic fields (EMFs) at home and at work is giving cause for increased "official" concern. They are another unseen pollutant that can be harmful to the chakras and health. Checking your environment for EMFs is very easy to do with a small portable radio. Set the receiver to the AM waveband, but do not tune it to a broadcasting station. Turn up the volume. Move close to an electrical appliance such as an answerphone, mobile phone, television, microwave oven, or ring-main circuits and sockets—an increased buzzing noise will indicate an electromagnetic field. Ensure that you do not sleep or work near such pollution—your head chakras are especially vulnerable.

BE NATURAL

Static electrical charges build up on synthetic materials such as clothing, carpets, plastics, and electrical equipment. These are particularly

Mental health
The workings of the mind are linked with the physiological processes of the body. Persistent negativity invites dis-ease. Persistent positivity maintains well-being.

Physical health
Your physical body will benefit from reducing your exposure to synthetic materials and machine-generated electromagnetic fields. Wear natural fibers and limit your exposure to environmental pollution.

harmful to the chakras. Try to wear natural cotton, hemp, wool, silk, or linen clothing. Eat organic food, and try to buy toiletries made only from natural ingredients. Artificial perfumes and chemical cleaners (such as bleach) severely affect chakra functions. With a little thought we can change our shopping habits, and our health. Also, to enhance the connection of your minor foot chakras to the Earth, why not spend a few minutes walking barefoot each day?

FOOD FOR THE CHAKRAS

The body requires a variety of fresh foods to maintain health. To keep the chakras in peak condition, it requires foods in all the colors of the chakras. For example, if the base chakra is underactive, red-colored fruits and vegetables should be eaten. Conversely, if it is overactive, red-skinned fruits, particularly hot red peppers and spices, are to be avoided. Make a list of all the red and orange fruits you can think of—these give energy to the first and second chakras. Yellow citrus fruits are acidic and stimulate excretion on both the physical and psychological levels, whereas bananas are "smoothies" that calm and balance the solar plexus chakra.

Eating lots of green vegetables regulates the entire metabolism, and also has a balancing effect on the heart chakra. Blue and purple fruits and vegetables could be said to have evolved on a higher level in order to empathize with the higher fifth, sixth, and seventh chakras. However, your diet must take into consideration your overall needs and should not become an obsessive pursuit of only chakra-enhancing foods—that would be just as harmful as a poor diet.

Artificial chemical food colors do not have the same effect as natural biological colors, so avoid eating them wherever possible.

WAYS TO FLOURISH

Try to replace the things in the left-hand column with the more positive, life-enhancing things in the right-hand column, as follows:

Hatred ⟶ Love
Abuse ⟶ Forgiveness
Despair ⟶ Hope
Moodiness ⟶ Laughter
Alcohol ⟶ Fruit juice
Fast food ⟶ Organic vegetables
Sugar ⟶ Apple
Coffee ⟶ Spring water
Bleach ⟶ Natural cleaners
Tranquilizers ⟶ Relaxation exercises
Antiperspirant ⟶ Natural perfume
Sleeping pills ⟶ Herbal teas
Gray/black clothes ⟶ Colorful clothes
Fluorescent light ⟶ Daylight bulb
Watching television ⟶ Walking
Recorded music ⟶ Live music, or just singing

LEFT: *The colors of the chakras, from base to crown, are reflected in the foods we eat. To activate or balance a chakra, eat foods in its color. To calm a chakra's overactivity, avoid foods in its color.*

ABOVE: *Alice Bailey was an orthodox Christian before the direction of her life changed and she became an esoteric writer and teacher.*

Color rays

Alice Bailey, a leading theosophist in the early years of the twentieth century, wrote extensively on esoteric subjects, particularly color rays. Her understanding of them was deep and complex, worthy of much study, but particularly complicated because she wrote in a way that employed a "blind" (a sort of paradoxical or reversed description), to keep information from the uninitiated.

Color rays are areas of influence in life. They do not necessarily appear in the aura. There are seven rays—creative energies emanating from a vast, mysterious central Sun or source. We are born under the primary influence of a particular ray. According to Bailey, rays affect human temperament and govern all life-forms. Each ray has both an exoteric color and an esoteric color, and each has a chakra attributed to it.

According to David V. Tansley, writing in *Chakras, Rays, and Radionics*, the rays that govern the etheric aspect of the chakras are as follows:

Ray 1	■	crown chakra
Ray 2	■	heart chakra
Ray 3	▢	throat chakra
Ray 4	■	brow chakra
Ray 5	■	sacral chakra
Ray 6	■	solar plexus chakra
Ray 7	■	base chakra

Tansley's work with radionics includes an holistic appreciation of chakras and rays, auras, astrological signs, tissue salts, Bach flower remedies, geopathic stress, miasms, and other similar subjects. From such a perspective of interweaving energies, we could more accurately describe ourselves as "hue-man" or "hue-wo-man."

THE MEANING OF THE RAYS

Here is an introduction to the many levels of understandings associated with the rays. To find your own ray, you should consult a radionics practitioner.

Ray 1 is red. It represents will and purpose. The hue-man of this ray approaches life through force of will and is often a leader, soldier, explorer, or ruler.

Ray 2 is blue. It represents love and wisdom. This person expresses compassion, patience, and serenity and may be a nurse, healer, teacher, or wisdom holder.

Ray 3 is yellow. It represents creative, active intelligence. This type of hue-man has a clear intellect, is adaptable and efficient. It is the ray of the philosopher, scholar, and businessperson.

Ray 4 is orange. It represents harmony through conflict. Strong affections and good artistic ability, together with courage and joy, make up the complex temperament of these people. They make good entertainers, artists, gamblers, musicians, and designers.

Ray 5 is green. It represents science or knowledge. It gives independence but also impersonal and harsh critical faculties, tempered by common sense. These people may be drawn to science, engineering, or medical research.

Ray 6 is violet. It represents idealism or devotion. The violet ray makes people full of intense likes or dislikes. They may be altruistically spiritually dedicated on the one hand, or fervently nationalistic and militant on the other.

Ray 7 is indigo. It represents order or ceremonial magic. It gives perseverance, discipline, dignity, and the ability to plan. It is the ray of the priestess or priest, healer, church minister, shaman, astrologer, and spiritualist. Indigo is said to be the ray of the New Age of Aquarius.

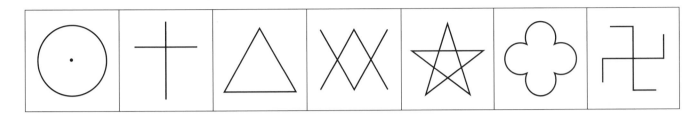

ABOVE: *A radionics practitioner may use these symbols of the Seven Ray Energies to pendulum dowse and analyze a patient's rays.*

RAY MIXTURES

To complicate matters, we may have more than one ray influencing different levels of our temperament. For example, Florence Nightingale would have had a strong blue ray (healing) with red ray influence (will and purpose). Martin Luther King would have had a dominant red ray (will and purpose) with violet (idealism) and blue (love/wisdom).

The rays also have negative aspects. Adolf Hitler would have had a primarily violet ray (militant fanaticism) plus red (tyranny) and some blue (indifference to others and poor self-image).

Have you ever met someone with whom you feel immediately at ease? New Age awareness might say that this is a Karmic connection, but maybe the connection is also through having similar ray influences.

DAY TO DAY

On our planet of colored light, the light rays go through a 24-hour cycle influencing both our temperament and our chakras. When we awaken at dawn, the dominant color is blue, which gradually takes on a turquoise hue, turning to green around noon. During the afternoon, the color changes from yellow to orange. As evening approaches, the red ray of the setting Sun predominates. At dusk, many shades of mauve and violet are apparent, eventually deepening into the indigo blue of night, and merging into dark magenta while we are sleeping.

LEFT: *The intensity of natural light changes throughout the day, surrounding us with colors that affect our mood and energy levels.*

VISUALIZATION EXERCISE

Sit outside (in natural surroundings) or imagine a place that you know well. Visualize yourself experiencing all the color changes that would take place from dawn to noon, to sunset, to night. Feel these colors of nature enriching your chakras.

Reflex chakras

Reflexology was rediscovered in the United States at the end of the nineteenth century. It is a therapy that uses the application of pressure to the feet or hands to treat various disorders. It was initially called zone therapy because the soles of the feet were divided into five perpendicular and four horizontal zones. Certain areas of the feet appear to be connected with body organs, as if the feet are a map recording them. In this book, however, we will confine our reference to identifying the chakra reflexes.

In reflexology, the arch of the foot represents the spine, and mirror positions may be plotted and treated on the feet as spinal reflex points of the chakras. You will need to visit a trained reflexologist to obtain a full treatment, but your own chakras can be balanced by self-treatment of "color pressure" to your feet. This can be achieved through thumb pressure and visualization of the

required color, or by using a small, smoothly pointed piece of tumbled crystal of an appropriate color to exert pressure. Begin with your right foot, moving from the crown to base chakra reflexes.

COLOR ACUPUNCTURE

Although it is not possible to treat yourself with color acupuncture (a practitioner will use colored filters or gemstones in conjunction with a low-voltage intense beam of light—not needles), you may still use a piece of tumbled crystal to give color to the foot reflex chakras, in the same way as a reflexology treatment.

COLOR IN YOUR HANDS

There are color reflex chakra points on your hands, too. Hands can be treated in the same way as feet, and are easier to reach! The hand chakra areas are shown in the illustration opposite, with their appropriate colors.

Lines on the hands of a human fetus start to be visible 15–17 weeks after conception.

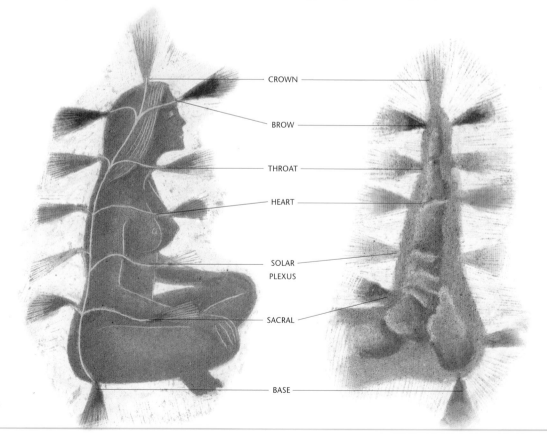

CROWN

BROW

THROAT

HEART

SOLAR PLEXUS

SACRAL

BASE

RIGHT: *Massaging reflexology points on the foot is believed to balance energies and stimulate physiological processes.*

HAND COLOR EXERCISE

This is great fun! You need a set of at least seven colored felt pens, or oil pastels, and two sheets of plain paper, each one large enough to accommodate your hand and a 2in (5cm) border around it. Place both hands, one at a time, on the paper and draw round them. Close your eyes, focus on your right hand (this reflects your life), and imagine what colors are on the hand. Then open your eyes, and quickly fill in the right hand outline with color.

Close your eyes, focus on your left hand (this is the potential with which you were born), imagine what colors are on this hand, open your eyes and quickly fill them in on the outline.

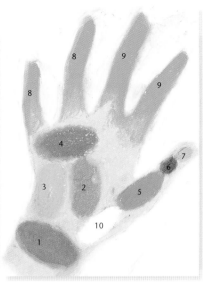

KEY
1 BASE: OVARIES, PROSTATE
2 SACRAL: KIDNEYS, ADRENALS
3 SOLAR PLEXUS: SPLEEN, LIVER, INTESTINES
4 HEART: HEART, LUNGS, THYMUS
5 THROAT: NECK/THROAT, THYROID
6 BROW: FRONTAL BRAIN
7 CROWN: INNER BRAIN
8 EARS
9 EYES
10 PANCREAS, BLADDER

NOTE: THERE ARE NO CHAKRAS FOR 8, 9, AND 10

HOW TO INTERPRET YOUR DRAWINGS

Reflect upon the information on the meanings of color given on pages 64–67 and on the meaning of the rays given on page 74. These will be your main guide. Here are some additional meanings.

Red		sexual energy
Orange		pranic energy
Yellow		mental abilities
Green within the outline		knowledge
Green outside the outline		nature connection (green fingers—a good gardener!)
Blue		Spirit, spirituality, higher guidance
Violet		inner transformation
Violet or gold		the soul
Pink		unconditional love
White		connection to God, Goddess, Creator

Center of palm	*your core energy*
Index finger	*dominant energy*
Lots of lines	*much energy*
Isolated areas of color	*disjointed chakra flow*
Overemphasis of one color	*dominant Ray*
Lack of particular colors	*related chakras need work*
Colors outside the outline	*awareness of auric energy*

Consult the illustration of the hand chakra areas to see if you have placed appropriate colors on the chakra areas. If so, they are extremely well balanced.Ideally your two hands should be in balance, showing all the colors, with colors moving from wrist to fingertips and a strong-looking area of color in the center of the palm (soul).

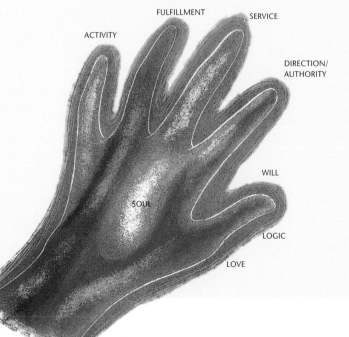

FULFILLMENT
ACTIVITY
SERVICE
DIRECTION/ AUTHORITY
WILL
SOUL
LOGIC
LOVE

Chakras and sound

Our chakras are actually part of a great "sea" of cosmic energy. Because of this, they respond readily to the primal vibration of sound. Myths in many cultures say the universe was created by sound. The Egyptian god Thoth was believed to have created the world with his voice. In ancient Egypt, Rome, Greece, Tibet, India, and Central America, vibration was understood to be the origin of life. Because chakras have this intrinsic affiliation with sound, many different ways of working with them have been developed over the ages. These include the use of mantras, bija-mantras, chanting, toning, singing, specific musical scales, and instruments.

Mantras

The Sanskrit word "mantra" is made up of two words: "man" (mind) and "tra" (instrument). Mantras are traditionally used to balance the chakras. Although the name originates in the East, mantras are also used extensively in many religions, including Christian prayer, to focus the mind. Mantras are short phrases that are repeated rhythmically either aloud or inwardly.

EXAMPLES OF TRADITIONAL MANTRAS

Om mani padme hum.
(God is a precious jewel in
the Lotus of my Heart.)

TIBETAN

Om tat savitur varenyam bhargo devasya
dhimahi dhiyo yo nah pracodayat.
(We meditate upon the adorable light of the
Creator. May he guide our understanding.)

GAYATRI MANTRA (HINDU)

Shemaa Yisrael Adonai Elohenu Adonai Eihad
(Hear, O Israel, the Lord is our God,
the Lord is one.)

HEBREW INVOCATION

Some invocations have acquired mantric value by repetitive use. For example, "Holy, holy, holy, Lord God Almighty." The affirmations given in Chapter 3 become mantric if repeated with the intention to transform yourself. A mantra needs to be said in its original language, not a translation, because the sound of each letter has a value and a vibration. Care should be taken to pronounce each syllable, being aware of lips, tongue, jaw, and throat as you do so. Vowels are an expression of the divine (so sacred in Hebrew that they were once spoken only by priests), and consonants are an expression of humanity.

BIJA-MANTRAS

These are "seed" sounds connecting us to the source of all manifested life. The bija-mantras are intoned aloud, or (unlike the vowels in the exercise) focused inwardly and silently during meditation to still the mind. They ascend through the chakras in the following order (phonetic sound in brackets): LAM (larm), VAM (varm), RAM (rarm), YAM (yarm), HAM (harm), KSHAM (k'sharm), and OM (ah-ooommm—see page 80). If you practice yoga asanas (postures) and know which chakras are being affected according to the body position held, you can visualize the appropriate bija-mantra and color for the chakra. This greatly enhances the power built up in your body during yoga.

ABOVE: *Thoth, Egyptian deity of learning, creator of languages, and divine scribe. He carries a pen to record judgment when the gods weigh the hearts of the deceased.*

RIGHT: *Many different methods of using sound to work with the chakras have been developed over the centuries. The chanting practiced by these Buddhist monks in Thailand is one way of creating a positive energy flow.*

Great power
is liberated
through careful
pronunciation of
all words. This is
particularly so for
the bija-mantras
associated with the
chakras. Native
American teachings
say, "Never name a
disease, since that
will give it power
over you."

SOUNDING VOWELS

Begin by learning these vowel sounds, watching yourself in a mirror so that you can slightly exaggerate the different shapes your mouth makes. Pronounce the sounds a number of times until you are familiar with them. Do this starting with UH as your lowest note, moving up one note of the octave for each chakra. If you have musical knowledge you can then sound the notes suggested as follows.

Letter	Sound	Chakra	Equivalent musical note
"u"	sounds like "UH"	base	deep C
"o"	sounds like "OO"	sacral	D
"o"	sounds like "OH"	solar plexus	E
"a"	sounds like "AH"	heart	F
"i"	sounds like "EYE"	throat	G
"a"	sounds like "AY"	brow	A
"e"	sounds like "EEE"	crown	B

Focus on each chakra in turn, with your eyes closed, and repeat the sound aloud a number of times, working up to five minutes on each chakra. Try to make each sound soft, but powerfully vibrating. Finally, listen to the silence.

THE SACRED OM

The ageless word "Om" carries with it a very potent vibration built up through repetitive sacred use. It embodies activation in the cellular membranes of the throat and head, and in the associated major and minor chakras. Additionally, as the main activating bija-mantra for the crown chakra, it forms a vibrational gateway reconnecting one's core essence to the source of Creation. To sound it correctly, make an "Ah" at the front of the mouth (wide open), moving to "oooo" (lips as an "o"), to "mmmm" (lips closed—try putting your finger to your lips to check that they are vibrating). Then try it again, pressing your fingers on your ears to block out the sound. Softly repeat "Om" many times. Use Om to calm yourself before meditation, listen to the silence between each repetition. Eventually, if you can hold this state without distraction, you enter into the ultimate state of bliss, which in Sanskrit is called *Samadhi*.

The Om symbol represents the states of sleeping, waking, and dreaming, separated from transcendence by the veil of illusion.

ABOVE: *The Sanskrit symbol for Om. The dot at the top represents the transcendental state, the crescent below is the veil of illusion, and beneath is the symbol of the states of sleep, dreaming, and wakefulness.*

ABOVE: *Each sound has a particular vibration and effect. This Brahmin man is making a peaceful spiritual greeting in front of a temple at Paryari Hill, Maharashtra, India.*

Chanting

Chanting is a part of esoteric tradition. We chant to enchant—to move into a magical space where we become the sound, and fall into the rich, comforting environment of human voice frequencies. All the chakras benefit from chanting.

A HARMONIOUS RELATIONSHIP

Emotions affect our chakras. The seed thought of an angry moment, for example, causes reactions in body chemistry and the chakras, some of which allow the thought to descend to its grossest manifestation, and consequently out come angry words. Although feelings are released by words, the body suffers chemical upset and pranic energy loss caused by internal tension. The chakras drain energy from the physical body to preserve their energy needs.

Meditation or mantras deflect anger and transform its consequences from negative to positive. Of course anger has its place, but in this world of tense living it is worth saving anger for important matters. To transform anger, it must first be felt inside, then two things happen. First, change in the quality of the anger occurs. At this point it may be possible to detach from it. Second, the intensity behind the anger moves the vibration in the only direction it can go, upward. Speech originates from another level of consciousness—a higher chakra with a cool, calm assertiveness. So the old adage that advises "taking three deep breaths before speaking, if angry," has reason behind it.

This way of dealing with emotion is based on the principles of Indian Shaivism, which are unlike those of Western psychotherapy. Some Western methods urge a release of anger by shouting or nonaggressive body movements, but away from the therapist's consulting room this type of therapy often fails to transmute anger and move it upward through the chakras.

SOME WAYS OF CHANTING

One way to use chanting is to work regularly with mantras. You do not need to undertake long periods of spiritual training to use them.

Their repetitive nature quickly saturates consciousness, enabling movement from everyday stress to expanded levels of consciousness, which, with practice, can be held for longer periods of time. This facilitates ways of dealing with emotions, so that chakras begin to resonate with your body. You do not need to be a wonderful singer to chant. What you are doing is making yourself come into resonance—a very natural thing to do.

GREGORIAN CHANTING

This is a harmonious type of ecclesiastical chanting, usually in Latin, developed in about 1000CE when large cathedrals started to be built and choirs began to sing at distances of, in musical terminology, a fourth or a fifth from each other, moving along in perfect parallels. Plainsong is similar but sung in unison. Both make excellent relaxation music when you are doing visualization, because the musical composition contains beautiful harmonies that will encourage beneficial brain patterns.

OVERTONE CHANTING

One example of overtone chanting is the deep bass baritone sound produced by the Gyume Tibetan monks. Since 1433CE they have used structured chants for protection and self-generation. They undertake up to 13 years of training to master the technicalities of three-note major chords, creating a very deep bass note with an inspiring range of harmonics.

LEFT: *When purchasing a Tibetan singing bowl, select the one that sounds most harmonious, because this will be balancing the needs of your chakras.*

RIGHT: *A novice Tibetan
monk practices chanting,
tuning in to universal
energies to seek a higher
state of consciousness.*

Toning for the chakras

Where in your life did you stop singing?
Where in your life did you stop dancing?
*Where in your life did you lose enchantment
with story—particularly your own story?*
*Where in your life did you start to feel
uncomfortable with silence, particularly
your own sweet sacred silence?*

UNKNOWN NATIVE AMERICAN HEALER

Every organ, bone,
and tissue gives
out a healthy
frequency of
vibration—we
have the ability to
project the correct
vibrations to
imbalanced parts
of the body and
chakras using
our own voices,
particularly by
the use of toning.

There is a great difference between singing and listening to someone else singing—as much as the difference between eating and watching someone else eat. Toning is very different from chanting and mantras. It is the sound of your body and soul expressing themselves, and does not have a coherent meaning because it is nonverbal, relying primarily on vowels produced with a nasal sound.

Toning was rediscovered by Laurel Keyes, an American who researched sound in the 1960s. It is an ancient method of healing that helps to restore people to their harmonic patterns. It releases the natural flow of energy and allows it to move through the chakras and the body.

HOW TO TONE

First of all refer back to the pranic breathing on page 12—it is a great help to be able to breathe well. Then, when you are breathing correctly, sit or stand comfortably and begin to tone. Breathing out, push your tongue against the roof of your mouth, behind the teeth, directing the flow of breath through your nasal passages and at the same time make a humming "mmmm" noise. Next make lots of different vowels sounds (a, e, i, o, u), moving your mouth into exaggerated shapes. See how easy it is—now you are toning! Have fun and don't let your mind get in the way. The point of learning toning is to explore free expression and improvisation. It can be helpful to allow your hands and body to move as you practice. Regular toning releases tension in the throat and the tone produced is enriched with its harmonics that may be heard as several sounds at the same time (multiples of the fundamental).

Sometimes they are high "trilling" sounds, a bit like birdsong, a number of octaves above the low notes, because of sound waves at different frequencies and intensity (amplitude). Although toning is so simple it can have amazing effects:

• It improves breathing. Deep breathing "massages" the organs below the diaphragm, assisting the base and sacral chakras in their work.

• It moves energy from the solar plexus chakra up through the heart chakra to the throat chakra.

• When making the nasal sounds (overtones) the rising vibration begins to activate head chakras. As this happens it brings the cosmic-charged energy in the brain into resonance with the ascending Earth energy at the alta major chakra.

• It activates all eight bones of the skull (eight notes make up an octave on a keyboard), repatterning the cerebral spinal fluid flowing through the spine that gives "messages" to the rest of the body. This is self-healing, and improves chakra strength. Chakras are very receptive to sound vibrations that encourage a two-way flow of energy to take place.

• Toning can be done anywhere—you don't need to be able to sing—you are playing the instrument of your own body.

• Fifteen minutes of toning a day beneficially affects heart, respiratory rate, flow of blood, brainwaves, and more. The sound always goes where it is needed.

FREE EXPRESSION—DANCING WITH LIGHT

A wonderful way to "nourish" your chakras is to feed them with a color, and beautiful, harmonious music (see pages 88–9). Do this exercise during the hours of darkness. You can either use an electric lightbulb in a particular color, or make a focus of a colored candle, flowers, and other objects in a particular color, setting them out on a colored cloth in the center of the room.

1 Play the music. Stand very still, getting in touch with your inner energies. Breathe deeply, imagining you are inhaling the color that you have selected.

2 Sense the music drawing color to the place in your body where it is most needed.

Begin to move that part of your body. For example, if you have a lower back problem, start to move your pelvis.

3 Allow the music to flow into the rest of your body. Experience the exhilaration of spinning around, or stillness as you hold a particular position. Be aware of how the music loosens your movements so that you use all the space in your room—lying and moving on the floor, or stretching up to the ceiling.

4 The chosen piece of music will take you to a natural conclusion to the dance. When you have finished your movements, lie down for a few minutes. Your chakras are now harmonized, refreshed, and recharged.

According to laws of vibration and acoustic proportion, an organism can be brought into resonance with its appropriate sound frequency. Every bone, muscle, and tissue of the body has its own particular frequency. Each chakra also has its own resonance. This has great implications for the future of sound healing and its application to the chakras.

LEFT: *Dervishes dance to hypnotic chanting, a devotion practiced at prayer meetings in the Islamic mystic movement known as Sufism.*

Beneficial and harmful sound

*"I do not wish to amuse my audience,
I wish to make them better."*

GEORG FRIEDRICH HANDEL

Although taste in music is a very personal thing, there are certain pleasing keys, rhythms, and instruments that will encourage the whole body to come into resonance through the chakras.

The way that sound is heard through the ears is complex. Part of the hearing mechanism in the inner ear involves about 16,000 minute hairs that change a sound into an electrical impulse to be taken via the auditory nerve to the brain. Loud sound, such as overamplified music, actually causes the little hair cells to stop working, leading to hearing reduction. Particular care should be taken to avoid loud sound during pregnancy, because the baby's ears become fully developed by the fourth month of pregnancy and damage to hearing could result.

Music can be soothing or stimulating to us, and to plants, animals, and insects. A spider can hear sound through its eight legs. Spiders have small hairs on their legs, which also help them to tell whether the ensnared insect in the web is going to be the right size to eat, or whether it is going to be harmful to them. Experiments show that a spider will respond to a particular piece of music if it contains the same vibration as its prey.

For the most part, music at normal volume is beneficial to us. Its psychological effects are profound. Compositions by Mozart have been used in an experiment to show the effect classical music can have on enhancing learning abilities and calming children's behavior at school.

When choosing Western classical music for relaxation or work upon particular chakras, consider the musical key it is written in as well as the composer's intention behind the "essence" of the music. As a general guide, the following keys will be beneficial for the chakras: C for the base chakra, D for the sacral chakra, E for the solar plexus chakra, F sharp for the heart chakra, G for

EXERCISE: LISTENING WITH YOUR WHOLE BODY

This is the way to really resonate to music with the whole of your body field (aura and chakras). Ensure that you will not be disturbed by intrusive sound such as the telephone or doorbell. Play a piece of music (classical is best for this exercise) that you are not very familiar with, lie down, and close your eyes. Let the low notes be heard around your base and sacral chakras, the medium notes at your heart chakras, and high notes at the crown chakra. Allow sudden, crisp notes to work on your solar plexus. During any pauses in the music, focus on your brow chakra—you may see many colors there or you might wish to make sounds yourself, thereby working on the throat chakra.

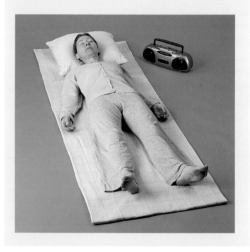

the throat chakra, A for the brow chakra, and B flat for the crown chakra.

According to Laeh M. Garfield in *Sound Medicine* (Celestial Arts, 1987), cool fifties-style jazz could overwhelm the sixth and seventh chakras if they are too open; loud, upbeat music with juxtaposed rhythms such as boogie woogie, hard rock, and heavy metal over-stimulates the base, sacral, and solar plexus chakras. Reggae lightly opens the second and third chakras, and aboriginal drumbeats open the entire chakra system.

LEFT: *Musicians perform for an Indian prince. Music is used in every culture to create the right tone for ceremony, celebration, and relaxation.*

Indian ragas are complex arrangements of vibrant traditional elements, usually built on seven tones, but with many fine subdivisions. Ragas often use a drone instrument such as a shruti box or a tamboura as a background accompaniment. The drone sounds something like a bee and induces quiet contemplation as the notes "play" upon all seven chakras.

The diatonic scale comprises the seven white keys within an octave on a piano. They resonate with chakras, colors, and notes as follows: First chakra: red, C; Second chakra: orange, D; Third chakra: yellow, E; Fourth chakra: green, F; Fifth chakra: turquoise blue, G; Sixth chakra: indigo/purple, A; Seventh chakra: violet/white, B.

The chromatic scale (the 12 notes of the black and white keys within an octave on a piano) is the one with which we are most familiar in the West. Again, there are correspondences with the chakras: the notes resonate to colors that provide the basic color for each chakra and the blend of colors that move between them. The colors are linked to astrological signs, as shown in the box below.

OTHER MUSICAL SCALES

A five-tone scale, called the pentatonic, is the oldest and most universally used. You can hear it when just the black notes are played on a piano keyboard. Chakra music written using this scale—known as "Primasounds"—is available in New Age stores.

The ancient Greeks used seven different scales, called Ionian, Dorian, Phrygian, Lydian, Mixolydian, Aeolian, and Locrian. Each scale had a very different effect on the body, and they may have been used in healing temples to work on specific chakras.

Note	Chakra	Color	Astrological sign
C	base	red	Aries
C sharp	base	red-orange	Taurus
D	sacral	orange	Gemini
E flat (D sharp)	sacral	orange-yellow	Cancer
E	solar plexus	yellow	Leo
F	solar plexus	yellow-green	Virgo
F sharp	heart	green	Libra
G	heart	green-blue	Scorpio
G sharp (A flat)	throat	blue	Sagittarius
A	throat	blue-violet	Capricorn
A sharp (B flat)	brow	violet	Aquarius
B	brow	violet-red	Pisces
C (next octave)	crown	white/gold	None

Infrasound (below human hearing levels of 20 hertz downward) produced by natural movements such as breaking waves, sands of deserts, grasses blowing in the wind, is thought to be an important guidance system for migrating birds (as well as Earth magnetics).

RIGHT: *Making direct contact with the Earth will allow you to share its vibrational energy.*

BELOW: *Dolphins are thought to possess emotional intelligence and seem to receive joy from their natural habitat.*

The magical sounds of nature

Deep peace of the running wave to you,
Deep peace of the flowing air,
Deep peace of the quiet Earth,
Deep peace of the shining stars.

CELTIC BLESSING

We have come a long way in our abilities to reproduce music electronically. Yet despite this, our chakras yearn for the peaceful nourishment of natural sound, for music is indeed a food. Legends tell of great Greek musician healers who could tune in to the inner harmony of a person and heal with a single note on their lyre. Often, the real inner essence of sound is lost when it is recorded, so try to listen to "live" bands, orchestras, and natural sounds as frequently as possible.

There is a great deal of difference between hearing and listening. Hearing is nonselective and does not require focusing. Our listening may be somnolent (sleepy), or it may be pro-active and highly energized. For example, when we are in the countryside, our state of listening can be sensitized to a point where one minute sound is distinctly audible within a whole concert of natural sounds. Proactive listening includes noticing the sounds between the

sounds. But remember that silence is important too. Refer back to the exercise for listening with your whole body on page 84—is it possible to do it if you are sitting in a peaceful garden? If you find it difficult, first tune in to the fundamental sounds of nature one at a time, and learn to be enraptured by the sound of birdsong, the wind in tall trees, or water moving over pebbles in a brook. Natural sound is so very important because, as with nonverbal music, it brings the right side of the brain into balance with the left. This in turn balances the action of the chakras around the head.

LISTEN TO THE EARTH
Here is a simple way to ground yourself if you are feeling stressed. You will feel energized throughout your body. Lie face down on the ground in a quiet place outside—this puts all the chakras at the front of the body in touch with the Earth. Energy exchange at the front of your chakras is needed to protect the physical body. By giving yourself to the Earth in this way, you help to dissolve overprotectiveness. Breathe more slowly—try to achieve such a relaxed state that you can feel a vibration coming from the planet itself. Listen to the Earth. You may perceive an inner sound. (The entire body, when relaxed or in meditation, vibrates at an inaudible frequency of around 8 wave cycles per second.) When you are ready to finish, turn over onto your back—this opens

the front of the chakras to the cosmos and allows any rigidity of energy in your back to dissolve into the Earth. The energies at the back of the chakras show the degree to which life experiences are held in fixed patterns. Rigidity of energy was described by Wilhelm Reich (an investigator into energy – see page 11) as "horizontal banding." It restricts the chakras in their function of moving energy freely up and down in the physical body. The result of this restriction may cause physical problems from backache to heart disease.

INFRASOUND
Even sound we cannot hear has an effect on our chakras—sometimes we feel the frequency as a vibration deep in the body, for sound waves can temporarily change the structure of the impermeable outer layer of skin.

Working with the elemental beings of nature
Occasionally, people who become particularly sensitized to the energies of Nature begin to feel "at one" with elemental beings (sometimes called the sylphs of the Air, undines of the Water, salamanders of the Fire, and gnomes and fairies of the Earth). To experience nature qualities more fully, sit by flowing water and ask

for it to happen—it may be that you will go into a spontaneous meditation and become part of the water, or you may see beings of water as energetic points of light, or you may even see the beings themselves. Everyone's experience is different; some people find it easier to do than others.

The nature essences of places are called devas. They are perceived as a particular type of good energy. Sometimes, clairvoyants see enormous landscape devas or angels that care for the land in their vicinity and act as mediators between the Earth and other levels of consciousness. Devas appreciate the attention of caring humans, and they are often the reason we are drawn back, time and time again, to a particular natural place that we love.

HUGGING A TREE
Rediscover how to be as spontaneous as a child—rush up and hug a tree! After a while, turn and rest your back against the trunk. Tune in to the life-force of the tree. If it is springtime, try to sense the sap rushing up to the new leaves as a movement of energy in your spine.

TRADITIONAL CHANT OF THE AMERICAS

Tierra mi cuerpo
Earth my body

Agua mi sangre
Water my blood

Aire me aliento
Air my breath

Fuego mi espiritu
Fire my Spirit

This chant is usually accompanied by drumming and rattles. For the most part, Native Americans have not lost their deep connection to the sacredness of the Earth. They refer to Father Sun, Mother Earth, and Sister Moon. Their cultures support a shaman who, when someone is ill, acts as a mediator between the worlds, treating the body with local herbs and bringing the patient's aura and chakras into balance through ceremony and ritual.

Blue whales have the loudest voices in the ocean, but their songs are usually at such a low pitch that humans can't hear them. The sound carries hundreds of miles, and it is thought that the whales track their location by timing the reflection of sound waves from mountain ranges under the ocean.

LEFT: *Trees are towers of living energy. Visualizing this energy rising upward along your spine can revitalize your chakras.*

ABOVE: *Aboriginal paintings look abstract to the uninitiated. Artists often paint accompanied by songs that invest them with spiritual power.*

Sound is one of the first senses we experience in the womb, and under normal circumstances, it is the last sense to leave us as we die. Some enlightened musicians use harp music to help terminally ill patients to die peacefully.

RIGHT: *Drummers play at a funeral in Ghana. Sound is used in many cultures to summon deities and mark rites of passage.*

Singing the Earth into being

My brother the star, my mother the Earth,
My father the Sun, my sister the Moon,
To my life give beauty, to my body give strength.
To my corn give goodness, to my house give peace,
To my spirit give truth, to my elders give wisdom.

UNKNOWN INDIAN SHAMAN, NEW MEXICO

Creation myths from around the world honor sound as a beginning. Often the Creator would manifest the Earth and then think of objects to create, vocalizing the sound for the object, creating its frequency, and bringing it into being. The Bible states: "In the beginning was the word." The Hindu Veda declares: "In the beginning was Brahman with whom was the word." Australian aboriginal people describe the "songlines" by which their world was created. This power of sound to create life is used by us today to recreate health by reducing the stress, even at deep cellular levels, that causes illness.

"TUNING" CHAKRAS FOR HEALTH

Listening to a live playing of the following musical instruments will enable the appropriate chakras to come into resonance. Recorded nondigital music played through good-quality analog equipment is almost as effective.

For the base chakra

Deep, low notes produced by an organ, drums, or double bases are felt as a deep resonance at the base chakra. If you are listening to recorded music, it should only be loud enough to create a gentle vibration in the body organs. Very loud sounds are detrimental to chakras.

For the sacral chakra

To balance the emotions at this center listen to viola music, chords played on a guitar, and an early stringed instrument called a lute.

For the solar plexus chakra

Loud brass instruments will jolt and clear out any unneeded "dead" energy that has accumulated

in the chakra. The saxophone is recommended because its sound is not too harsh. Classical guitar playing will calm this chakra.

For the heart chakra
To develop unconditional love at this chakra, listen to the sublime sounds of classical violin or piano sonatas, particularly by Mozart.

For the throat chakra
The flute is excellent for balancing this chakra, because it lifts the lower energies up through the heart chakra to transmute and express them at the throat chakra.

For the brow chakra
This is stimulated by the visions that harp music can induce.

For the crown chakra
Harmonics created by Tibetan or crystal singing bowls will work beneficially upon the crown chakra. Surprisingly, any of the drone instruments will affect the chakras right though from the base to the crown.

Listening to an orchestra
When we listen to a beautiful piece of music played by a full orchestra, with its huge range of harmonics, all our chakras are affected. Sound vibrations passing through them will be "colored," or it could be said that they are given an added dimension, so that as the sound permeates into the physical system, it goes exactly where it is most needed. Of course, just listening to music, even for long periods of time, does not change the nature of illness in the way that medicinal drugs do. But a life without music could be gray and grim. Music intentionally chosen for chakra balancing will have a gentle and stabilizing effect upon illness. Together with other complementary therapies it supports overall health of the body.

Some sound therapists are able to analyze the voice to discover specific sound frequencies that are stressed or missing in a patient. The frequencies can be reintroduced to the brain to bring about positive health.

SCANNING CHAKRAS WITH SOUND
You will need to do this exercise with a friend. Its purpose is to pick up imbalances in your friend's chakras by using your voice.
1 Begin by standing about 4½ft (1.5m) apart, facing each other.
2 "Tune in" to your friend's energies by standing quietly for a while.
3 Take one deep breath. Upon the "out" breath, sing one fairly high note (that is easily within your capabilities), keeping your palms directed toward your friend's head.
4 Slowly, but within the same breath, bring your palms down, focusing the power of sound toward your friend.
5 With practice, you will notice subtle changes in the quality of the note that you are making, and so be able to locate imbalanced chakra areas.
6 This method can be used to make a simple diagnosis, which can then be followed by any of the chakra balancing methods recommended in this book. Afterwards, check the chakras again with the sound of your voice to see if any change has occurred.

Note: If you possess a large, single-pointed quartz crystal, the power of your voice may be "amplified" by holding the crystal in front of your mouth and singing through it.

The ancient Greek mathematician and philosopher Pythagoras made a simple instrument called a mono-chord, by which he figured out ratios and harmonies of numbers. He is said to have heard the "harmony of the spheres"—the sound vibration that planets and stars make as they traverse space.

New awareness

The fact that you have been drawn to read this book means you may be someone who is making subtle auric field energy connections to assist personal transition into the next stage of human and planetary development. People who experience this awakening may be described as "multidimensional light beings," whose auras have expanded to include additional chakras located within and above their head.

Links to sound, light, color, and crystals help to develop potential within us. They increase our abilities to cope with the potent surge of newly awakened energy through our chakras, which help to transform them into "centers of power."

The living library

At cellular level, our bodies hold a record of life experiences. We are a living library! New ways of perceiving our universe, from microcosmic to macrocosmic levels, indicate that in some way everything is related. Every plant, stone, and animal is here on this planet for a reason. The stars we see at night have an effect upon us. Our library is constantly growing.

The Earth has its own library. Some people say our chakras are the major key to accessing information stored in the Akashic Record—a record or library of all that is, all that has been, and ever will be on planet Earth. Others say that many dimensions twist, turn, and interpenetrate themselves, making a coherent field of experience available through different types of altered consciousness such as those from meditation, hypnosis, dreams, shamanism, and hallucinogenic states. Whatever belief system we choose to follow, chakras are central to our understanding because they are the doorways (portals) of opportunity through which altered states can safely be accessed.

RIGHT: The Akashic Record is a record or library of all that is, was, and ever will be on Earth. Some people believe that we can access all this information through the chakras.

BEYOND THE SEVEN CHAKRAS

It could be said that our journey, or spiritual goal, is to travel a path to our human heart within, and to bathe in the fountain of unconditional love. So far we have studied the traditional Vedic teachings on how the chakras correlate to areas and functions of the physical body. Traditional Indian yoga has taught us about the system of the seven major chakras and their predominant color vibrations that match the colors of the rainbow in the order in which they ascend through our body. We have also seen how chakras form entry and discharge points—portals—for energies to flow between the aura that surrounds us and our physical body.

In this chapter we are going to explore beyond the seven chakras, and the possibility of reaching a new state of consciousness.

THE EARTH SPEAKS

Crystals shine out with star energies.
Herbs hold the vibration of planetary energies from our solar system.
Trees strengthen the connections between Earth and heaven through the energy grids of manifestation.
Flowers "kiss" the angelic energies.
Devas sustain all seen and unseen life on planet Earth with the cooperation of the elemental beings of Earth, Air, Fire, and Water.

Unity—everything that is in creation exists within you, and everything that exists within you exists in creation

KAHLIL GIBRAN—*THE EYE OF THE PROPHET*

Be aware of chakra energies as you plant seedlings or harvest crops. Native American teachings, although highly divergent from tribe to tribe, honor the nature guardians of plants by singing to them at these times.

A CHANGING WORLD

It is becoming increasingly obvious that our connection to the cosmos is changing. Our actual knowledge, as well as our deeper intuitive understanding of the universe, is very different from that of our ancestors. At this moment in our planet's history, we are being flooded with more and more cosmic energies. Through our chakras, we can select energies that are needed for positive human and planetary growth at this time. As these energies increase the possibilities for human evolution, we begin to understand that the seven-chakra system, appropriate as it has been for the last two thousand years or so, is like a chrysalis. From it we will emerge into a new consciousness that carries with it a glorious body of light, like the wings of a beautiful, ethereal butterfly.

We need to begin to look at the potential of transmission beyond the chakras, which can connect us to the more interpersonal and interdimensional nature of ourselves as beings of light. Present-day mystics speak of fundamental evolutionary changes taking place, even at DNA level, as our awareness expands with the subtleties of the further chakras, and we start to key in to "wheels within wheels."

The 12 major chakras and their qualities

I have floated in the universe of the infinite and flown in the upper air of the imaginary world. There I was close to the circle with its divine light; here, I am in the prison of matter.

KAHLIL GIBRAN, *THE EYE OF THE PROPHET*

The additional chakras just mentioned are the Earth star, the navel or hara, the causal, the soul star, and the stellar gateway. They are placed within the sequence of the seven chakras as shown here.

The Earth star chakra is placed wherever our aura touches the ground. Every step we take anchors our Earth star to the planet. The rising interest in environmental concerns, "green"

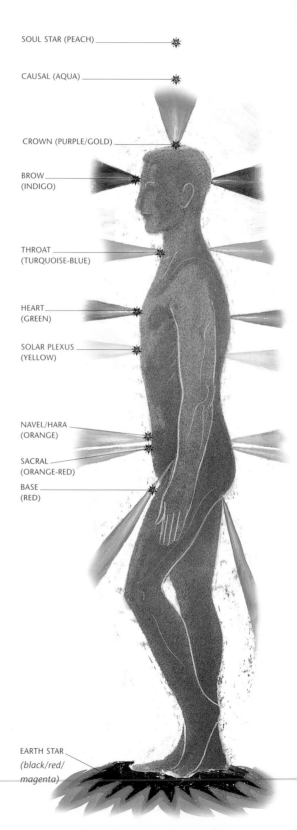

STELLAR GATEWAY (SILVER) ————— ✴
(actual position
is about three to
four feet above aura)

SOUL STAR (PEACH) ——————— ✴

CAUSAL (AQUA) ———————— ✴

CROWN (PURPLE/GOLD) ———— ✴

BROW ———
(INDIGO)

THROAT ————
(TURQUOISE-BLUE)

HEART ———
(GREEN)

SOLAR PLEXUS ——
(YELLOW)

NAVEL/HARA ——
(ORANGE)

SACRAL ———
(ORANGE-RED)

BASE ————
(RED)

EARTH STAR ———
*(black/red/
magenta)*

ABOVE: *T'ai chi is an excellent way to move positive energy through the chakras and the physical body. It is based on a system of free-flowing coordination and harmony, and will help to bring balance and stability where they are needed.*

it is the point where the outside influence of other people's chakras is first registered, causing our reactions. In addition, it is where we process our personal links to the Akashic Record. It is on the outer limit of auric sight and is perceived as a soft aqua-blue sphere of light.

The soul star chakra's name is self-explanatory. It is positioned beyond the limits of our auric field and can be described as a chakra because it is the place where the soul enters at conception, and which becomes the initial abode of the soul immediately after death. This gateway chakra is connected to the aura by a thread of light that appears to open, when the body is dying, as a tunnel to experiences beyond death. A number of ancient cosmologies, including Egyptian, say that at death we become stars in the universe.

The stellar gateway chakra is actually a cosmic gateway accessible to all enlightened beings. It is believed that on our journey through life, and as a soul, we maintain a constant connection with the center of all that is—the Creator. The stellar gateway opens to cosmic consciousness, taking us to unimaginable realms of blissful love wisdom.

politics, and ecology over the past four decades is an indicator that Earth star chakras are becoming active for many people.

The navel (hara) chakra is just above the sacral chakra, but below the navel. In Eastern terminology it is known as the hara. Many people in the West have embraced Eastern teachings, such as yoga, t'ai chi, chi kung, judo, and shiatsu, which all move energy through the chakras and body. For them, the navel chakra is usually more developed than the sacral chakra and may perform some of its functions, but at a slightly higher frequency of vibration.

The causal chakra sits at the outer limits of the aura, above the head. It performs an important function with a flow of energy that centers on our assemblage point, a shamanic term indicating the dimension in which our consciousness is held. The causal chakra is described as an interpersonal chakra, because

BELOW: *The Egyptian Book of the Dead contains secret words that enabled the pharaoh's departing soul to break through four openings, or veils, into the sky, so that he could ascend to the stars.*

Being in the flow

Sometimes we may just not be able to put our finger upon what is wrong with us. We are not exactly ill, but our energy is low. Imagine a scale of health, somewhat like an old-fashioned barometer. When energy is low, it hovers at a midpoint, occasionally dropping down to sickness or moving up into optimum health. Another way of describing this feeling is being "out of the flow."

Imagine the source of all life as a generative ray of energy from deep space. In accordance with natural law, it enters the body through the crown chakra and descends to Earth through the feet. We humans are the only species on Earth able to transduce (step down in power) energy in this way. When chakras get out of alignment, energy flow is diminished, and physical illness eventually results. Of the two main chakra functions, physical health and spiritual personal growth, the universe primarily endeavors to meet the needs of the latter, while the essence at the physical core battles with our fragile bodies to maintain our life on Earth. All the meditations and visualization exercises worked with so far endeavor to bring you back into the flow, in touch with the source of life.

THE HIGHER SELF

The causal chakra has another function, the development of what is referred to as the "higher self." This is an aspect beyond conscience (a person's sense of what is right and wrong), because conscience is conditioned, molded, and at extremes manipulated, by the type of society we live in. The higher self knows at a very deep level the right action to take in any circumstances, because the higher self is an expression of our

LEFT: *Being in touch with the source means that our connection with universal energy allows us to come truly alive. Being out of touch can make us feel "low" or unwell.*

soul. The way to increase the positive action of the causal chakra and the higher self is to act selflessly, without conditions or hidden motives, particularly those for personal gain. This is the path of unconditional love. When this behavior is repeated time and time again in life, when unselfish gestures are made continually, a bond naturally links to the higher self at all times. This is an important teaching at the core of the world's great religions. Only the words are different, and their interpretations clouded from the seeker.

Eileen Caddy, cofounder of the Findhorn Community, an intentional spiritual community in Scotland, looked at herself in the mirror one day and said quietly, "I must learn to love myself if I am to learn how to love others."

UNIVERSAL LIGHT-BRIDGING MEDITATION

This is an unusual meditation because it is most effectively undertaken in the standing position. The purpose is to generate the fullest possible bridge of energy between your Earth star chakra connection to the Earth and your stellar gateway to the cosmos. Just as electrical wiring will only support a certain current, the physical body will only support a certain maximum flow of energy, so do this meditation only for a short time, until you feel ready to extend it.

1 Stand outside with bare feet in a quiet place on some grass. Activate all seven major chakras, visualizing your spine as a column of bright light. Allow this light to grow stronger and, breathing deeply, let the light completely fill your body.

2 Send a strong "root" down from your feet through your Earth star chakra to the center of the Earth.

3 Raise your arms and ask to be filled with golden white light. Imagine that you are becoming so tall that you can touch the stars. Continue breathing in this bridge of light until you are full.

4 Lower your arms, with your palms facing outward at shoulder level. Now breathe golden white light into your heart chakra, feeling it expand.

5 From your heart chakra, visualize sending out light to the four compass directions of the Earth, turning around anticlockwise to do this. Start in the east, turn to the north, then west, then south. Imagine the light clearing all the places on the Earth where there is pollution, despair, or fear.

6 Feel joy as you know that this work has been done, and gradually release the bridge of light.

BELOW: *Individual spiritual development brings a responsibility to contribute to the spiritual development of the planet. Light-bridging sends our chakra energies to the corners of the Earth in the form of cleansing light.*

New consciousness IS here, but like a seed it needs nurturing so that it flowers in mainstream expression.

Holistic living—our responsibility to the Earth

Light is in the darkness of my thinking
Light is in the light of my being
Light is in the colors of my chakras
Light is in the sound of my speaking
Light is in the form of my body
Light is from the source of all Creation.

Holistic healthcare is a therapeutic approach that treats the whole person—body, mind, and spirit. Living holistically means honoring our presence on the Earth by taking from it only that which we need. It is about sorting out needs from wants.

Chakras are key to how we can live placidly and happily in touch with our environment, whether in the city or the country. Everyone is born with unencumbered chakras, but from early childhood onward, each chakra acquires negative states of consciousness. These are caused by a variety of life experiences, but

particularly abuse, loss of a loved one, or pain. However, we can choose to transform the chakras by consistently and intentionally increasing pure light energy passing through them. To illustrate this point, we must return to the seven major chakras, which are the main centers to work with at this stage. Negative states and their positive counterparts will be listed in order. If you see yourself described by any of the words on the list, it is an important indication that a chakra requires balancing. In this way, you can begin to acknowledge, accept, and integrate all levels of your "beingness."

TYPICAL NEGATIVE AND POSITIVE CHAKRA STATES

1 Base chakra
– A tendency to be self-centered, violent, greedy, angry, and insecure.
+ Connection to the natural world, stillness, courage, patience, and control of the body will balance this chakra.

BELOW: *Free yourself from negativity by integrating with your surroundings, living in harmony with the energies of the Earth.*

2 Sacral chakra

– A potential to overindulge in food or sex. This person may live with confusion, jealousy, envy, and a desire to possess material wealth and objects.

+ Tolerance and working harmoniously and creatively with others. This person has the ability to change and assimilate new ideas, respecting others, and their opinions and needs.

3 Solar plexus chakra

– A tendency to take on more than one can assimilate. This person may place too much emphasis on power and fame. Emotions of anger, fear, and hate, perhaps directed toward someone, are likely to produce digestive problems if the solar plexus chakra is imbalanced.

+ Willpower, and authority tempered by intelligent and quick mental processes. Ideally, this person will give out radiance, warmth, humor, and laughter, but develop the ability to be cool, calm, and assertive when required.

4 Heart chakra

– If this chakra is severely out of balance, it can cause circulation and heart difficulties for the physical body. This person's natural expression of love may be repressed, and may be causing emotional instability.

+ Learning compassion, acceptance, openness, harmony, and contentment leads to unconditional love and will counter any negativity in this chakra.

5 Throat chakra

– This person may use words to hurt others, or may be unable to communicate his or her own truth, leading to depression and an inability to sing or speak with joy in the voice.

+ Learning true communication with others and creatively using the voice to praise, and to speak truth, peace, and wisdom, will overcome any negative aspects in this chakra.

6 Brow chakra

– People who are out of touch with their third eye, or brow chakra, will often experience a lack of concentration, fear of the unknown, cynicism, tension, headaches or migraines, bad dreams, phobias, and feelings of detachment from the world.

+ Developing inner powers of intuition, insight, imagination, clairvoyance, concentration, peace of mind, and wisdom will enlighten the brow chakra.

7 Crown chakra

– Severe trauma or senility can cause the crown chakra to be virtually inactive, which will eventually lead to death. Negative states experienced by someone with severe crown chakra imbalance include confusion, depression, alienation, and an unreasonable or ill-founded fear of death.

+ An active crown chakra opens to the causal chakra, the soul star, and the stellar gateway chakra, giving ultimate oneness with the infinite. Steps along this journey are the unification of the higher self with hue-man/ wo-man personality, divine service, wisdom, and perception of dimensions beyond space/time/usual consciousness.

SACRED LAWS OF GUARDIANSHIP FOR PLANET EARTH

Life Development of the positive states of consciousness that flow through the chakras automatically brings awareness of the unique place we hold as beings of rainbow light on the planet. Perform some act of kindness each day.

Love We often express this in many ways toward our families and our friends, but we should also express it toward any animals, plants, stones, or crystals around us.

Laughter When living fully with love, we resonate with joy, laughter, song, and dance to celebrate the Earth and all its creatures. Be spontaneous.

REINCARNATION AND NEW AWARENESS

Some people believe that great Earth changes in the coming years will mean that we are unable to reincarnate on Earth—thus the desire now to expand consciousness and "live lightly on the Earth."

The main Christian Churches in Britain joined to make a Millennium Resolution, giving each household a candle and asking them to light it at two minutes to midnight and read: "Let there be respect for the Earth, peace for its people, love in our lives, delight in the good, forgiveness for past wrongs, and from now on a new start."

Celtic people still celebrate a natural "mass" from earlier times called Lammas, or loaf mass, when the first ground wheat, made into small loaves, is shared and offered to the Earth Goddess, who has blessed the land with her abundance. The last stalks of wheat are made into a corn dolly that carries the energies of the land from the harvest through to the spring planting, ensuring the continuity of the cycle.

KEY

1 Root chakra: Lake Titicaca, Peru/Bolivia.
2 Sacral chakra: Mount Shasta, California, U.S.A.
3 Hara chakra: Nah Chan (Palenque), Mexico.
4 Solar plexus chakra: Uluru (Ayer's Rock), Australia.
5 Heart chakra: Aquarian Triangle centered on Glastonbury, England.
6 Throat chakra: Mount Fuji, Japan.
7 Brow chakra: Gunung Agung, Bali.
8 Crown chakra: Mount Kailas, Tibet.

RIGHT: *Chakra-flow around the planet, like the undulations of two great earth serpents, forms major Earth energy lines.*

The big picture chakras

The concept of the Earth as a mother was prevalent among many ancient peoples, and in classical Greek times she was known as Gaia. In the 1970s, a scientist named James Lovelock proposed a theory that the Earth is similar to a living being. It became known as the now-famous Gaia hypothesis, stating that the biosphere is a self-regulating entity with the capacity to keep the Earth balanced and healthy by controlling the chemical and physical environment. At around the same time, astronauts were giving us incredible pictures of the planet from space. Together, these two events caused a shift in consciousness toward the idea that the Earth, like other living beings, has chakras. These are shown on the chart, which gives locations that are representative of the type of energy or essence that sensitive people are able to pick up. The locations are also traditional sacred areas for the people living there.

PLANETARY AND EARTH CHAKRAS

Planetary chakras are part of a whole global energy grid, whereas Earth chakras are the more local ones, like major and minor chakras of the body.

We need to take care to ensure that we do not project our humanized chakra interpretations upon planetary and Earth chakras, for there are many forces beyond the realms of physical perception that interact with the planet. These include forces such as the elementals, devas, and nature spirits that are prevalent at the Earth chakras, and which give the chakras strong energetic characteristics. Planetary and Earth chakras have the intrinsic facility to clear themselves of pollution, in marked contrast to human beings. Although we hue-mans are normally born with a completely intact energy system, it can be a great struggle to maintain the health of our chakras and keep our pranic energy flowing throughout our adult life.

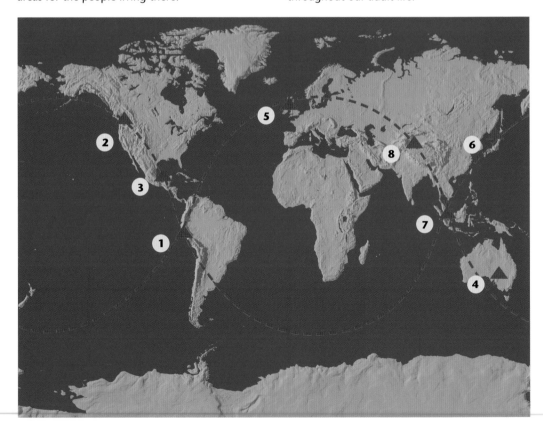

DISCOVERING CHAKRAS IN THE COUNTRY OR IN TOWN

In addition to the major Earth chakras, patterns of energy that correspond to chakras can often be identified in country or urban areas. By doing some research in old maps and history books, we may discover a sacred spring that was a site of pilgrimage—this could be a sacral chakra. In the country, look for the sacral chakra at ponds, lakes, or the confluence of two rivers. The tallest hill in the area, perhaps with an ancient grove of trees, may be the crown chakra; in a city it could be located at a cathedral steeple or important building.

The solar plexus chakra is associated with the element of Fire, so look on maps for furze (fire) or beacon hills. The throat chakra is linked to communication; in a town it may be the site of an old marketplace or the town hall. Study a map, and visit the places you locate to sense the "spirit of the land." In many instances, you will intuitively find the heart chakra of an area first. Confirm the feelings you have about a place by using dowsing rods or a pendulum (see pages 110 and 111).

CHAKRAS IN CATHEDRALS AND ANCIENT CHURCHES

Throughout the world, many religious buildings have been built upon ancient sacred sites. In Britain, the first Christian churches and cathedrals were constructed on sites that earlier beliefs had designated as being in balance with Earth's natural forces. The font inside the west entrance of many early cathedrals was frequently built over flowing underground water, once worshiped at ancient springs in quiet forest glades. Such buildings, conceived by skilled architects and master masons, have a precise overlay of chakra energies.

In a typical cathedral of early construction, the congregation enters by the west main doorway that is the base chakra. Baptism takes place at the sacral/hara chakra. People sit in the nave of a cathedral, where their emotions are heightened through the solar plexus chakra. The transept is the perfect crossing of the east/west and north/south, forming the heart chakra. This is often separated from the altar end of the cathedral by a rood screen that acts as a veil or gateway so that the heart love of the congregation and their inner intent gains entry through the throat. Of course, it is the choir, heard but unseen, that creates sacred sound. During mass or communion, people seek inner realization at the brow chakra of the altar rail. The priest alone intercedes as a channel for God the creator, blessing the sacrament at the high altar (the crown chakra) and taking it down to the altar rail for the people partaking in the service.

UNIVERSAL CHAKRA LINKING

Like our own chakras, Earth chakras are vortices of energy that receive and transmit information. There is so much disharmony on the planet today that many people are using prayer and visualization for Earth healing. The following exercise provides Earth healing for your own area, but could also be visualized over the world map. It is called "distant" healing because it is done from home.

Identify the main subtle energy focal point of your area, which in Earth healing is referred to as the hara, or sacral chakra. Light a candle, placing it before you or in the center if you are sitting among a circle of friends. Relax quietly for some minutes, releasing any "clutter" in your mind.

Focus on the inner light at your own hara or sacral chakra, then expand this light. Picture the place chosen and visualize a brilliant spiral of energy from the center of the Earth flowing up into it, and golden light pouring down. The energies meet and the place shines with bright light. As the power increases the light radiates through the area, above and below ground, enfolding everything in a beautiful loving glow.

The light spreads far beyond and joins up with the energy lines like a huge web of light surrounding the Earth. Now each Earth chakra, small and large, radiates light.

Gently focus back into your room. If you are doing this meditation with other people, hold hands, acknowledge each other with eye contact, then blow the central candle out together.

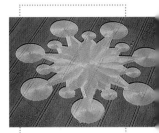

Seventy-nine percent of the crop circles in southern England form over areas that provide drinking water. Is a third of the English population drinking "messages in the fields," and the rest of the world getting a homeopathic dose through interconnecting oceans?

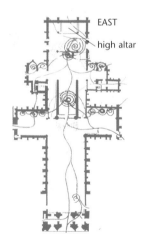

EAST
high altar

ABOVE: *In cathedrals, the high altar is placed at the east to face Jerusalem. It also focuses the energies of the rising Sun through the crown chakra. Some cathedrals have extra transepts at the brow containing small chapels, which are the minor temple chakras. Earth energies cross at the heart chakra.*

Babylonian priests from the third millennium BCE onward, observed the heavens. Many of the fixed stars and constellations were known and named by them.

As above so below

Ancient peoples recorded in stone their understandings of the cosmos. From around 3000 BCE, Neolithic "priests of light" began building the great stone circles of Europe, such as Avebury and Stonehenge in England. Monoliths of stone were placed to act as solar markers, measuring seasonal events connected with solstices and equinoxes. Pyramids in Egypt and temples in Central America were positioned to represent specific star formations or Earth energy flows. The ancient people of these places had a day-to-day working knowledge of both astronomy and astrology, which were taught alongside the science of human chakras. The pulse of the Sun and the stars was living in their physical bodies. Today, much of this deeper natural wisdom is being reawakened with the realization that spiritual science contains universal truths. We can access it when we make pilgrimages to sacred sites throughout the world.

CLEARING EARTH ENERGY GRIDS

Planetary and Earth chakras are positioned on the Earth's energy grids at multilayered intersections, creating vortices of power so attractive to

BELOW: *Stonehenge in the county of Wiltshire, in England, is connected to other nearby sacred sites along earth energy lines.*

hue-mans that we are drawn to the sacred sites on them. Earth energy grids are connected with our own subtle energies, but in many cases have become influenced by negativity within human consciousness. When we arrive at these places, if we intend it, we can form an interaction that will help clear the Earth grids. One of the best ways to do this is to use the Universal Chakra Linking Exercise on page 99.

ASTROLOGY AND CHAKRAS

One easy way to understand the influence of stars and planets upon us is to imagine a Ray of Creation coming from a central source. This ray is so powerful that it has to be transduced through constellations of stars, splitting it into many rays, before reaching the solar system. Our Sun acts as a lens to focus these rays from outer space, passing them through the planets and then to the Moon and Earth. The Ray of Creation is changed from one almighty ray to rays of many different frequencies of color, which are attracted to our human chakras. Ancient teachings give the following correspondences between chakras, planets, and astrological information (see opposite).

Chakra	Planet	Astrological Signs	Astrological Houses and Influences
Crown	Jupiter/Neptune	Pisces	12th: Challenges
Brow	Uranus/Saturn	Aquarius/Capricorn	11th: Objectives/10th:Profession
Throat	Jupiter/Mars	Sagittarius/Scorpio	9th: Intellect/8th: Death
Heart	Venus/Mercury	Libra/Virgo	7th: Partnerships/6th: Health
Solar Plexus	Sun/Moon	Leo/Cancer	5th: Love/4th: Family
Sacral	Mercury/Venus	Gemini/Taurus	3rd: Education/2nd: Possessions
Base	Mars	Aries	1st: Life

NOTE: On an astrological chart the position of the houses never changes, whereas the position of the signs does. What we have shown above is the "natural" house for the sign, but the actual position will vary in each person's chart.

STAR VISUALIZATION FOR THE 12 CHAKRAS

Science measures the light from the stars with spectrographic instruments that analyze the different colors produced to indicate which minerals are present. Similar minerals are on our planet, in our food, and in our bodies. Your own connection to the stars will be enhanced by this visualization of a different type of star at each chakra.

1 Sit or lie down and relax. Visualize being connected through your feet to intense blackness under the Earth.

2 Now see the rich, red-brown color of the soil and draw it toward your feet until it changes and becomes a shining bright red glowing star at your base chakra.

3 Move your attention up to your sacral chakra star, which glows orange-red, then on to the navel chakra, which emits a clear orange light.

4 The color gradually changes to clear bright yellow as it reaches the solar plexus chakra. It changes again to green at the heart chakra, becoming brighter and clearer as feelings of unconditional love pour into your heart.

5 The color changes again as it reaches your throat, the green becoming tinged with blue, turning to a turquoise-colored star at the throat chakra itself, glowing, sparkling, and spinning as thoughts are focused there.

6 Your brow chakra is a single bright white star in an inky-blue night sky. It slowly turns and beams light as attention is centered on a midpoint just above your eyebrows.

7 Now move to your crown chakra—see a star emitting purple and sparkling golden light resting gently on the top of your head.

8 The next chakra, the causal, shines starlike with a clear, aqua-blue light.

9 Moving to the limits of your auric field, now see the most beautiful peach-colored star softly glowing and sending its light to you. This is the soul star.

10 Finally, the mixture of colors you see coming from the stellar gateway is indescribably brilliant and can best be understood as silver sparkling light. You have connected with the stars, your chakras, and limitless love.

11 Return from whence you came, going back down through the colored stars of light, sealing each one in a circle of golden white light as protection. You pass through silver, peach, aqua, purple/sparkling gold, white/ indigo, turquoise, green, yellow, orange, orange-red, red, red-brown, then back into the Earth. But now your Earth star chakra has transformed from black into a magenta-violet star.

In thirteenth-century England the center of learning was the new University of Oxford. The first recorded chancellor of the university, Robert Grosseteste, accepted the teaching of astronomy–astrology as a supreme science for guiding all human activities, from planting vegetables to alchemy.

Chakras and sacred stones

Crystals are a precious gift from the Earth. Some crystals are as much as four million years old, yet their beauty and brilliance, especially when cut and polished, make them shine like nature's stained-glass windows. Through their color, shape, and form we may enter worlds within, without, and beyond, so that the boundaries of everyday life pale to insignificance.

A crystal is a uniform body, the atoms of which possess a regular geometric arrangement. This arrangement may, or may not, result in a regular external form. Again the number seven features here, for there are seven basic crystal systems: cubic, tetragonal, orthorhombic, monoclinic, triclinic, hexagonal, and trigonal.

Crystals and chakras

The balancing effect of crystals upon chakras and the body has been known since ancient times, when the art of the laying on of stones was practiced. Civilizations and races whose knowledge is not currently available to us passed the secrets of stones and crystals to the Egyptians about 12,000 years ago, and today we are relearning, by intuition and meditation, their many uses. Crystals are considered by many to be very much on the "cutting edge" of new healing, and even medical doctors are showing interest in their properties.

Quartz is one crystal that has up-to-the-minute technological applications. It is used in oscillators for precise vibrational frequencies, in capacitors for energy control, transmission, and storage, and for the purification of air through ionization. The scientific properties of quartz are those of reception, reflection, refraction, magnification, transduction, amplification, focus, transmutation, transference, transformation, storage, capacitance, stabilization, modulation, balance, and transmission, as well as being directional. Quartz can display full-spectrum light reception and polarization. Many of these important qualities are utilized when we balance chakras with crystals.

CHOOSING CRYSTALS

Crystals have a special relationship with chakras and are ideally suited to help balance, activate, or calm them. You may like to obtain a selection of small, polished crystals called "tumbled stones." If you can only afford a few stones, purchase pink rose quartz, purple amethyst, and red-orange carnelian. These will

give you a range of different energies to experience. You may like to hold your crystal or stone and draw energy through it, quietly sitting in a meditational state. Just by being in the presence of crystals, the energies of your chakras start to change. Clusters of amethyst crystals, for example, as well as acting like spiritual room fresheners, clear your aura and chakras too. Wearing crystals as jewelry is an obvious way of keeping their beneficial effect close to your body. Choose rose quartz for general balancing of the chakras, or clear quartz (rock crystal) for increased energy. Do not use factory-made Austrian crystal, because it contains lead impurities.

CHOOSING CRYSTALS FOR THE CHAKRAS

Choice is more accurate if done intuitively. Sometimes it will seem as if a crystal chooses you! The size of the crystal is not as important as the positive feelings it gives when held in the hand. Look for nicely shaped stones or crystals with no damage and of appropriate color, because there is a sympathetic association between stones (or crystals) and the same color vibration of various chakras. The chart on page 105 gives examples of healing and balancing stones and the appropriate colors.

It is unwise to use complicated layouts of crystals on the chakras unless you are a trained crystal healer. For general use, limit the number of chakra crystals to three at any one time. Placing crystals on the highest four chakras is not recommended. The best way to begin to understand how crystals attune to chakra energy is to use meditation to form a resonant relationship with the stones listed in this section.

RIGHT: *All crystals, whether clear or cloudy, crystalline or smooth, have a balanced internal structure and potential healing powers.*

RIGHT: *Crystals and plants encourage a good energy flow inside your home.*

ABOVE: *Before placing your crystals in a medicine bag, wrap them in red silk to protect them from damage and to maintain their energy field.*

> Obsidian is a volcanic glassy substance, and amber is fossilized tree resin millions of years old. Neither of these substances has regular arrangements of atoms, so is not classified as a crystal.

YOUR MEDICINE BAG

As soon as you have obtained some crystals that you want to carry around, it is helpful to make or purchase a medicine bag. This should be of natural material such as soft leather or cloth. From now on, you are the guardian of these crystals. Eventually you will need 7 or 12 chakra crystals (depending upon which chakra system you are using), 2 grounding stones (see below, right), and 3 small, clear quartz crystals.

CRYSTAL/CHAKRA EXERCISE

First wash three tumbled crystal stones (rose quartz, amethyst, carnelian) in cold water, then place them in front of you. Your hands have minor chakras: the left palm predominately receives energy, and the right palm predominately gives energy. This exercise concentrates on the experience of receiving energy from the stone, so with your eyes closed pick up a stone and place it in your left palm. Sit very quietly and just "tune in" to the stone. You may notice some kind of energy activation in your hand or arm. It could be tingling, pulsating, vibrating, hot, or cold. Whatever it is, permit the stone to work at a very deep level through your chakras and body.

Now inwardly ask yourself which chakra needs balancing with the stone. You will have an immediate desire to place it somewhere on your body or hold it to that area. Keep it there for a while, sensing a vibrant thread of light energy connecting you with the stone. When finished, transfer the stone to your right hand and open your eyes.

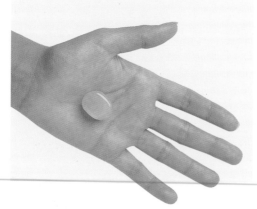

CRYSTALS IN YOUR HOME

If you prefer, you can keep crystals in a bowl or special place, or on an altar in your home. Some crystals, such as fluorite, calcite, celestite, and turquoise will fade if always left in strong sunlight. Crystals enjoy being with houseplants.

GROUNDING STONES

Channeling light and healing through the Earth star chakra

To overcome the "spaced-out" feeling sometimes encountered when working with crystals, you will need a grounding or earthing stone. Any stones or crystals that feel dense and heavy can be used for this purpose. Beach pebbles are ideal, because their energies are very clear. Black tourmaline or obsidian helps connect with the goddess essence of the Earth. Iron pyrites seem to draw us into the planet's crystalline iron core.

Once you have chosen a grounding stone, wash it and place it at your feet; or sit so that it is positioned at the base of your spine; or hold it in your hands. Become connected to it. Try to sense roots growing from your feet down into the center of the Earth. Be aware of light passing through your Earth star chakra. Once you can earth yourself in this way you can hold other crystals or place them around you, knowing that your awareness can always be brought back to the earthing/grounding stone.

CHAKRA	VISUALIZATION COLORS	PROPERTIES	HEALING/BALANCING STONES
Earth Star	Black/red (magenta when activated)	Spiritual grounding point, integration with Divine essence, and transmutation of fears.	Hematite and black tourmaline
Base	Red	*Muladhara*—gonads, pelvis, legs, and feet; physical grounding point.	Garnet, smoky quartz, red jasper, and obsidian
Sacral	Orange/red	*Svadhisthana*—adrenals and reproductive organs. Regenerative creative energy and tribal memories and origins.	Brown or blue lace agate, and bloodstone
Navel/Hara	Orange	*Hara*—kidneys, digestion, and absorption; physical sustenance and strength.	Tiger's eye and carnelian
Solar Plexus	Yellow	*Manipura*—stomach, spleen, pancreas, and liver. Development of mental and physical movement.	Topaz, peridot, amber, citrine, and gold calcite
Heart	Green	*Anahata*—heart, circulation, and lymph. Unconditional love, compassion, balance, and harmony with all creation.	Emerald, dioptase, rose quartz, ruby, rhodonite, and green jade
Throat	Turquoise/blue	*Vishudda*—thyroid. Verbal and artistic expression and protection.	Turquoise, sodalite, and aquamarine
Third Eye/ Brow	Indigo	*Ajna*—pituitary and center of nervous system. Eye of the soul, inner sight, and purification of thought.	Purple fluorite, malachite, lapis lazuli, sodalite, and amethyst
Crown	Purple and sparkling gold	*Sahasrara*—pineal. 1000-petalled lotus, strong double-helix vortex, gateway, expansion of consciousness, and connection with the Earth.	Amethyst, clear/golden rutilated quartz, and sugulite
Causal	Aqua	Receptive womb, conscious reprogramming, meditation, silent peace, universal concepts, and connection with the solar system.	Kyanite, moonstone, and celestite
Soul Star	Peach	Abode of the soul after death, bridge, channel, psychic cleansing, DNA activation, and connection with the galaxy.	Selenite
Stellar	Silver	Conscious intention, oneness, gateway, and connection with the universe.	Moldavite

Caring for your chakra crystals

Once a crystal comes into your keeping you become its guardian, and you need to know how to care for it. Of course it is essential to keep a crystal free from dust and static— it also has a surrounding energy field, equivalent to our aura. Both before and after use, cleanse the crystal's auric field by one of these methods:

- Wash it in fresh water
- Leave it in the sunlight or moonlight
- Pass it through the smoke of incense or a smudge stick
- Meditate and visualize your crystal being washed in a clear mountain stream
- Give healing to your crystal (for example Reiki healing)

DEDICATING YOUR CHAKRA CRYSTAL

When a crystal first comes into your keeping, get to know it, cleanse it, then hold it, saying,

"May this crystal work only with the power of Unconditional Love and Light, for the highest universal purpose of …" (* Here you add, in this example, "chakra balancing," or any other appropriate dedication.)*

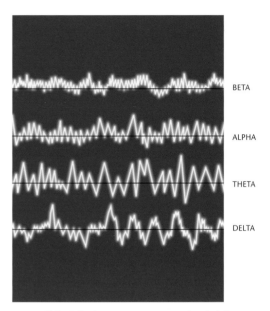

ABOVE: *Shifts in brainwave patterns cause chemical changes that induce altered states of consciousness. We may experience these as transitions between different states, such as sleeping and waking. When crystals are passed through chakra points, they can change these brainwave patterns.*

CRYSTALS FOR HEALING

It is known that brainwave patterns are altered when a crystal is passed through chakra points— there is an instantaneous flare of delta (unconscious) and theta (subconscious) activity. Could this be evidence for some intuiting mechanism in the consciousness of the human body recognizing and responding to crystals? Alteration of brainwave patterns causes chemical changes that induce altered states of consciousness. There is nothing unusual about these altered states, for we constantly move from one state of consciousness to another, particularly during the processes of sleeping, dreaming, and waking. Altered states induced by deep relaxation are very beneficial to working with crystals and chakras. Couple this with the energy channeled through a trained healer, and the effects may be felt as helpful physical change in the body.

The crystal layouts that follow can be used on yourself or a friend. Remember to cleanse all the crystals before and after use, and to dedicate them.

RIGHT: *A smudge stick produces pungent herbal smoke, which encourages any static energy inside a crystal to flow freely.*

LAYING OUT CHAKRA CRYSTALS

You will need three small, clear quartz crystals, called "single points," and an appropriately colored crystal for the chakra you wish to balance (see the chart on page 105).

As an example, let us assume you have chosen a small piece of green jade for the heart chakra. If you will be wearing clothing, try to wear white cotton. Prepare the room by lighting incense or using a smudge stick. Light a candle and, if you wish, say an affirmation or a prayer. Ensure there will be no disturbance and that you will be warm enough. Lie on a blanket or bed, and go through the relaxation exercise on page 21 if you feel stressed. Have the jade and the three quartz crystals close at hand, then arrange them in the center of your chest. Place the jade in the center with the three quartz crystals pointing inward to make a triangle. Remain with the crystals in place for up to 20 minutes, keeping relaxed.

If you do this exercise with a friend, ask him or her to read the relaxation aloud and slowly, then to place the crystals and jade in position. He or she should then sit quietly nearby until the crystals are removed.

THREE-CHAKRA CRYSTAL LAYOUT

Decide which chakras need balancing. They may be obvious, or you can use one of the methods in this book to help you choose. Do not attempt to balance more than three chakras at any one time, and unless you are experienced as a healer, do not place crystals on chakras above the throat. You will need two clear quartz crystals and your medicine bag of crystals from which to make a choice.

Prepare everything and relax in the same way as described in the previous layout above. When you lie down, put two quartz crystals in place, and grounding stones below your feet. When you are relaxed, place three crystals on the appropriate chakras. Stay relaxed, with the stones in position, for up to 20 minutes.

Crystals possess a regular structure, which emits stable and constant vibrations able to resist outside influences. They are referred to as a "free resonance substance," having a fixed and level pattern of vibration. The human body is a "forced resonance substance," having a fluctuating pattern of vibration. When a person is out of balance, especially during illness, the vibrations of crystals at the chakras, together with a focus of healing energy, can bring molecular activity into harmony by achieving resonance and balance.

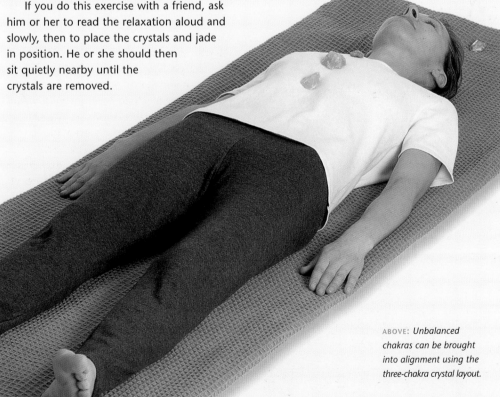

ABOVE: *Unbalanced chakras can be brought into alignment using the three-chakra crystal layout.*

Advanced chakra activation

Although you can safely balance chakras yourself, please note that only a trained healer should attempt to activate a chakra for another person. Generally, we suffer from a lack of energy throughout our chakras and physical body. The majority of conditions will respond when a healer sends a surge of appropriate energy through the body, and crystals will have a similar effect. Occasionally during healing and natural medicine treatments, "healing crises" can occur, where a condition seems to worsen for a while. However, this is only the body clearing out "debris," ready for cellular-level healing to take place.

All the layouts on this page should be used on one chakra at a time, after you have prepared the room and relaxed yourself. If you are unable to place crystals on bare skin, lie between two white cotton sheets. Alternatively, put a small piece of colored silk over the body area corresponding to the chakra you have chosen. You may put the silk on top of the white sheet. Next place the chosen crystals on top of the silk.

Each crystal layout energizes the chakra—to enhance this, visualize the resonant color and appropriate Indian symbol over the chakra area. (You will find the Indian chakra symbols illustrated at the beginning of each section in Chapter 3.) Breathe in the appropriate color. Exceptions are the layouts for the crown and soul star chakras, which are whole body layouts. With every layout:

- Cleanse the crystals before and after use
- Lie with your head to the north
- Place a grounding stone below each foot
- Drink pure water before and after doing the layout

If you are attempting to treat a physical condition associated with a chakra, please remember that the use of crystals should not replace medical treatment.

BELOW: *Activating the third chakra. White sheets allow the light energy of the crystals and yellow silk into the body.*

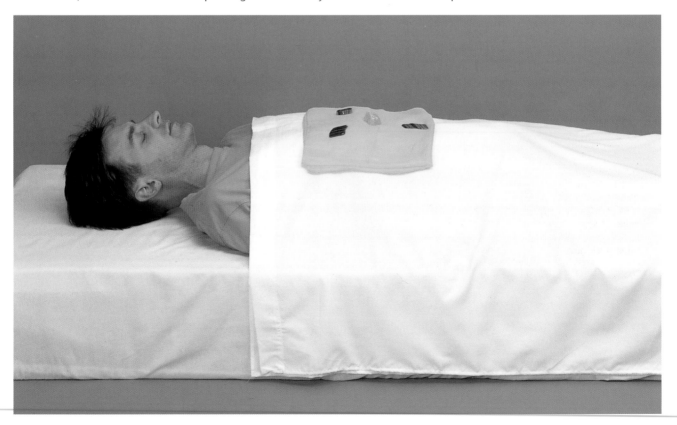

CRYSTAL LAYOUTS FOR THE CHAKRAS

Base chakra
1 herkimer "diamond" at center
4 black/green tourmalines
Use red silk

Sacral/Navel/Hara chakra
1 herkimer "diamond" at center
5 moonstones
Use orange silk

Solar plexus chakra
1 citrine/topaz at center
3 tiger's eye or iron pyrites
Use yellow silk

Heart chakra
1 herkimer "diamond" at center
3 green tourmalines/smoky quartz
3 rose quartz
Use pink or green silk

Throat chakra
1 turquoise at sternal notch
1 herkimer "diamond" either side
1 gem silica/turquoise/ chrysocolla at
  side of neck
Use turquoise silk

Brow chakra
1 herkimer "diamond" at center
1 lapis lazuli on brow skull protuberance
Use blue silk

Crown chakra
1 herkimer "diamond" on midpoint of sternum
1 quartz above head
1 quartz below feet
1 grounding stone below each foot
Use violet silk

Soul star chakra
1 herkimer "diamond" on midpoint of sternum
1 double-terminated quartz above head
1 quartz below feet
1 grounding stone below each foot
1 celestite cluster above head
Use white silk to cover the whole body
  if possible

Base chakra   Sacral/Navel/
                Hara chakra   Solar plexus
                                chakra   Heart chakra

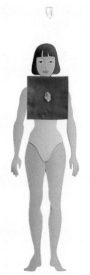

Throat chakra   Brow chakra   Crown chakra   Soul star
                                             chakra

Choice of pendulum

A pendulum is a very useful "tool" for your work with chakras. It enables access to all manner of information that the conscious mind would not have thought possible. The only limitation is that questions should be formulated so that they require only a "yes" or "no" answer. However, there is a need to disconnect completely from the outcome of the answer, because your mind can influence the swing of the pendulum.

A pendulum may be made from a variety of materials, although you may like to choose one made of beautiful crystal. However, it is essential to feel comfortable with whatever type is used. The pendulum will become an extension of your own subtle energy field, detecting, among other things, slight variations in surrounding subtle energy areas. When you have chosen your pendulum, wash it (if it is crystal), dedicate it (see page 106), and keep it for personal use only.

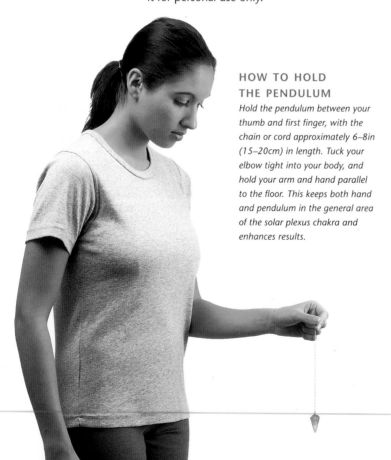

HOW TO HOLD THE PENDULUM

Hold the pendulum between your thumb and first finger, with the chain or cord approximately 6–8in (15–20cm) in length. Tuck your elbow tight into your body, and hold your arm and hand parallel to the floor. This keeps both hand and pendulum in the general area of the solar plexus chakra and enhances results.

HOW TO USE A PENDULUM

First, you must find out what your "yes" or "no" reactions are. Relax, take a few deep breaths, then hold the pendulum a little above your other hand (see the picture on the opposite page), and ask, "Is my name…?" (giving your own name). The pendulum should immediately react, swinging in a circle, either clockwise or anticlockwise. This is your "yes" response. Very occasionally, a person's "yes" response is a movement from side to side or front to back. Now run your hand down the length of the pendulum to bring it back to a resting position.

Now, find your "no" reaction. Ask "Is my name…?" (giving a false name). The pendulum should immediately turn in the opposite direction to the "yes" response. Practice for a while to make sure of the pendulum's responses by asking questions to which you know there is a "yes" or "no" answer.

ABOVE: *The pendulum amplifies energy flows. When you direct energy into the body by asking a question, the energy is echoed back to you through the pendulum's movements.*

DOWSING THE CHAKRAS

The technique involved in using a pendulum is known as dowsing. To dowse, it is necessary to build up an empathy with your pendulum, to make sure that the method is reliable for determining the degrees of activity of your chakras. Work systematically through each of your chakras asking, "Does this...chakra require balancing?" Another question worth asking is "Is this...chakra overactive?" or "Is this...chakra underactive?"

Avoid holding the pendulum over a chakra—instead, you should point a finger of the other hand toward and near the chakra. This ensures that the pendulum does not falsify the reading.

Record your results on a piece of paper, both before and after working, so that you can begin to see repeating or varying patterns of chakra activity. You can also detect and compare effects that the various methods

shown in this book have upon the chakras, by dowsing before and after carrying out any balancing exercises.

MAP DOWSING TO LOCATE EARTH OR PLANETARY CHAKRAS

You can use a pendulum to dowse over a map in exactly the same way as explained for the body chakras, working with questions that can only have a "yes" or a "no" answer. Slowly run the index finger of the hand that is not holding the pendulum over the parts of the town or area relevant to the questions, until the pendulum reacts as you ask, "Is this the...chakra for this area?"

If you choose to go outdoors to experience planetary or Earth chakras in the landscape, with a little practice dowsing rods will enable you to detect vortices of Earth energy and other energy flowing in lines and grids. Dowsing rods are often easier to use outside, because the wind can blow a pendulum or it can swing too much as you walk. Refer back to page 28 for how to make dowsing rods.

"Terrestrial zodiacs" have been discovered by dowsing methods. When plotted and joined on a map, ancient field boundaries, rivers, natural landscape features, and village names produce a landscape counterpart to the celestial zodiac signs. Research has been published on the Glastonbury, Nuthampstead, and Bury St. Edmunds zodiacs in Britain.

LEFT: *Hamish Miller, a British dowser, has used his skill with dowsing rods to map out an Earth energy line more than 200 miles (300km) long in southern England, linking sites such as the Avebury stone circle and Glastonbury Tor.*

How to use pendulum swing charts

An excellent way of supplementing "yes" and "no" answers is to use the charts on this page. It is a different method, so do not expect the pendulum to go around in circles.

Hold the pendulum as shown on the previous page, but commence by using the other hand to swing it backward and forward over the heavy dotted center line on the chart. Keep your mind focused on a specific question for which you desire an answer. Check that the question is precise and unambiguous. Eventually the pendulum will settle down to swinging in just one section of the chart. This is your answer.

HOW TO USE A CRYSTAL PENDULUM

Do this exercise with a friend. Never hold a crystal pendulum over a person, because it will immediately start to influence the movement of the chakra being dowsed.

1 Ask your friend to lie down. Kneel to your friend's left side. Hold your left hand a little above your partner's body, sense the general area of the chakra, and find its center with your middle or index finger.

2 With the pendulum in your right hand ask, "Does this chakra need balancing?" Work through each chakra, seeking "yes" or "no" answers. Then use one of the methods in this book to bring the chakra back into harmony.

RIGHT: *Use this chart to ask the pendulum which chakras are unbalanced, keeping your mind clear of any preconceived ideas.*

RIGHT: *Focusing on a particular chakra, use this chart to ask the pendulum about the energy qualities of the chosen chakra.*

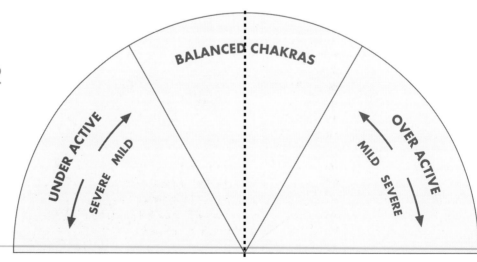

1

SACRAL
SOLAR PLEXUS
HEART
THROAT
BROW
BASE
CROWN

2

BALANCED CHAKRAS
UNDER ACTIVE
SEVERE MILD
OVER ACTIVE
MILD SEVERE

3

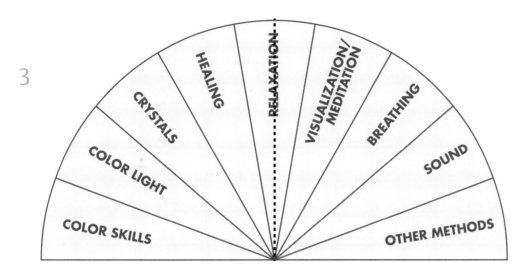

LEFT: *Ask the pendulum which method should be used to balance a chakra. Again, focus your mind on the chakra concerned.*

4

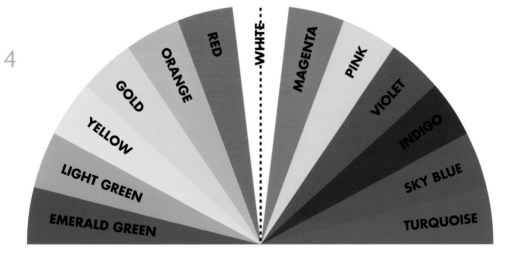

LEFT: *If you are using color therapy, ask the pendulum which color will activate a chakra, or which will calm it.*

5

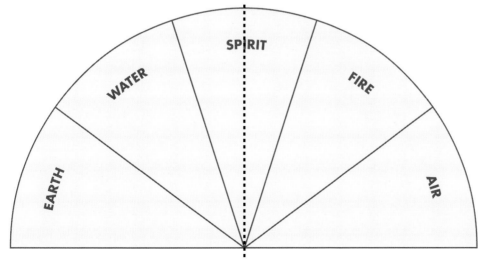

LEFT: *If you are using visualization, ask which elemental force to meditate upon to balance your chakra energies.*

Guidelines for healers

Many people have trained as healers in methods such as spiritual healing, Reiki, auric healing, pranic healing, and healing with crystals, color, or sound. The following guidelines are especially for healers working with crystals.

Remember that the energies of the chakras are actually incoming and outgoing spirals. Crystals are effective on both the physical body and/or the auric field. Before commencing a healing, observe the subtle differences in energy quality between the chakras on the front and back of a person's body. The back is often a reflection of a person's outer projection in the world and may be excessively rigid. The front is softer and more vulnerable, exhibiting inner feelings, and may put up defense mechanisms. During periods of spiritual growth, energies flowing through the head chakras are in a state

of adjustment as they become finely attuned. Therefore, do not work on any of these higher chakras unless you have been professionally trained in the use of crystals.

CHOICE OF CRYSTALS FOR HEALING

When selecting crystals to use on chakras, have a very clear intention of working in harmony with the highest universal purpose. Remember that you are a channel through which healing may pass, and which will become focused through the crystals and the recipient's chakras. Always try to use a balanced set of similar-size crystals, chosen from the 12-chakra illustration (see page 92) or the pages of chakra correspondences in Chapter 3. Alternatively, depending on your intuition, use crystals of a single type, such as quartz.

WORKING ON EACH CHAKRA

1 Create a sacred space in a way that is appropriate by lighting a candle, cleansing the room, and praying or meditating. Establish your own "grounding" connection to the earth and be ready in "healing mode." Cleanse and dedicate the crystals to be used (see page 106).
2 Ask for guidance or assess what is needed for the person by dowsing with a pendulum, or scanning.
3 Ask to be a channel for healing to balance the chakra. Put the crystals in place.
4 Increase the healing vibration.
5 Move healing energy as guided. Draw from both "earthly" and "heavenly" realms.
6 Allow what needs to be.
7 Remove the crystals, immediately placing them in a bowl of pure water.
8 Seal the encodement of healing and auric field of the recipient with a hand movement that, to you as a healer, symbolizes Divine protection.
9 Acknowledge and give thanks for both your guidance and the crystals. Finish with a prayer if it is within your spiritual tradition.
10 Stabilize body energies and subtle energy flows of both yourself and the recipient, then close down to an appropriate level.
11 Ensure that the recipient is comfortable, then wash your hands and cleanse the crystals.

BELOW: *Healers connect universal energy with the life-force of the person being treated, enabling him to heal himself.*

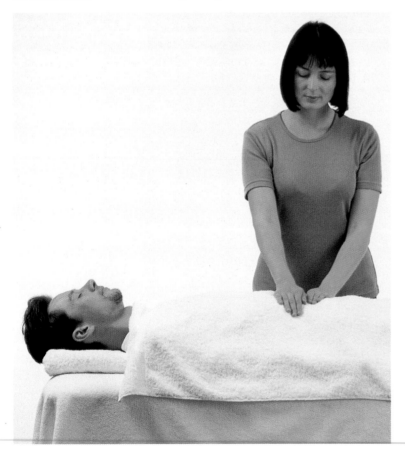

A	B	C	D	E	F	G
Clockwise spin	Anticlockwise spin	Still point	Oval	Star	Backward and forward	Side to side

GO WITH THE FLOW

An alternative to yes/no dowsing is to dowse for chakra energy patterns with a pendulum. Hold the pendulum as for previous methods, point a finger of the other hand toward the chakra, and simply ask, "Show me the energy pattern of this chakra." The pendulum will respond in one of the ways shown in the illustration above.

Draw a chart to show each chakra and its reaction, copying the layout of the example shown below.

INTERPRETATION

A and B: balanced chakras usually alternate in their direction of spin. C: the still point means that you have "locked into" the center of the vortex. You may feel a very strong pull on the pendulum, even though it is not held over the chakra, but away from the person's body. Try positioning the pendulum slightly to one side. D, F, and G: indicate an unbalanced chakra. E: a star pattern indicates a very powerful flow of pranic energy, transmutation or channeling of spiritual energies.

BELOW: *A chakra flow chart. Use a different colored pen to record a person's results on three separate occasions, on one chart. In this way, you will build up a diagnostic picture of his or her chakra well-being.*

CHAKRA FLOW CHART

	incoming energy to chakra	outgoing energy from chakra	outcome
Crown	~~anticlock~~ weak/~~strong~~/erratic ~~large~~/medium/small circle	~~anticlock~~ weak/~~strong~~/erratic ~~large~~/medium/small circle	balanced
Third eye	~~anticlock~~ weak/~~strong~~/erratic large/medium/small circle	anticlock weak/strong/~~erratic~~ large/medium/small circle	Receiving transmutative energies and endeavoring to utilize them
Throat	~~anticlock~~ weak/~~strong~~/erratic large/~~medium~~/small circle	~~anticlock~~ weak/~~strong~~/erratic ~~large~~/~~medium~~/small circle	balanced

Shamanism and energy balance

In this section we explore a little-known aspect of the chakras that has been revealed to the author through shamanic work. The terminology is very different from main New Awareness teachings. Thus we speak of a "journey of power" undertaken by a "warrior."

Shamanism is a traditional art that may involve a "journey of power" to enter an altered state of consciousness in order to access other dimensions of reality. The word "shaman" or "shamanka" (a female shaman) is Siberian in origin. A shaman is independent of organized religion and may either focus upon healing or be a warrior shaman seeking power and liberation. Indigenous peoples often support one or more shamans in their town or village, who look after the needs of the community. Apprentices are always drawn from local people. Now, however, for a few Western people, shamanic states occasionally happen spontaneously as an inner movement or shift of consciousness while dreaming, or going through serious illness or near-death experiences. Such events may cause recall of past lives, remembering the sorcerer, magician, or wise leader within. This calling may prompt a leaving behind of everyday life, while seeking explanations from the natural world of plants and "power" animals.

THE ASSEMBLAGE POINT

The assemblage point is a shamanic term. It is possible to think of it in terms of a chakra or a vortex. Its natural position is at the center of the chest or back, slightly to the right. However, the assemblage point is different from a chakra in that it positions the body into a particular time and space reference—usually everyday reality. It is like having a map grid reference to know where you are. A shaman seeks to move his or her assemblage point, along with personal identity, into other realms. It is not necessary for a shaman to take drugs to undergo this experience.

For ordinary people, dreaming allows the assemblage point to shift around in a spontaneous, although somewhat chaotic, manner. Some people can become totally immersed in a superficial everyday reality, in which they are unable to visualize or remember their dreams, because their assemblage point has become immovably fixed, perhaps by social conditioning or peer group pressure. For other people the assemblage point is positioned precariously in their physical body and is unable to maintain its optimum position, which will eventually lead to illness.

With practice, another person's assemblage point can be located to ascertain if it has shifted from its natural position. The lower it drops from this location, the less vital energy will be possessed and processed. The chakras will not function fully as energy exchange centers, and the person will be lethargic, sucked into personal comfort scenarios, or even physically ill. If the point drops below the navel, death will occur rapidly. When the assemblage point is stabilized, the chakras will work to their optimum capacity.

During shamanic journeying or dreaming, the art of moving your own assemblage point can be practiced. It may take a lifetime's apprenticeship to control this at will.

LEFT: *For generations, Native North American shamans have helped to heal the sick, and have foreseen the future, by entering an altered state of consciousness and communicating with the spirit world.*

SENSING THE ASSEMBLAGE POINT

For this you need to work with a friend. His or her assemblage point can be found with a pendulum or dowsing rods, but it is easier to find it following the method described below. Using what is known as "second attention" (somewhat like another sense, which develops as "personal power" when we are aware of the magical world of nature around us), it is possible to sense either individual chakras or the assemblage point within your friend's auric field.

1 Shake a rattle or create a steady drumbeat to change your everyday focus, as well as to change the energy of the room. Such instruments and other vocal sounds are used by shamans to clear negative energies before commencing their "journey."

2 Ask your friend to stand up and look straight ahead. Stand to your friend's right side.

3 Form your left hand into a soft cup shape in order to feel/sense the end of the assemblage point in the area of your partner's shoulder blades at the back.

4 Form the thumb and fingers of your right hand into a tight bunch and sense/feel for the bundle of energy lines entering the front of your friend's body. Feel for the area of maximum energy. This is the current position of your friend's assemblage point.

MOVING YOUR OWN ASSEMBLAGE POINT

If your friend's assemblage point is out of alignment with the body's center line (or dropped low down), your friend could consider rectifying it for him- or herself. Moving another person's assemblage point should never be attempted. However, a genuine healing shaman from an indigenous culture would know how to do it directly and responsibly.

Only working personally and indirectly to balance the chakras (as shown in this book), with crystals, color, breathing, and sound should be attempted and this could automatically improve the position of the assemblage point. Ideally, this book should be read slowly and the exercises practiced diligently for at least a year, so that

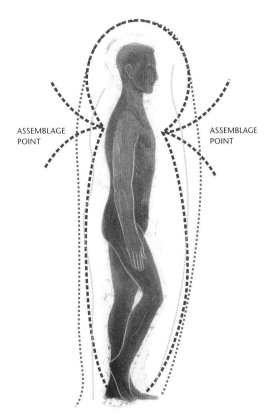

ASSEMBLAGE POINT   ASSEMBLAGE POINT

they become more a way of life than a linear thought process of learning. With increased movement of subtle energies through chakras, the assemblage point will then spontaneously shift and usually stabilize, resulting in a more favorable location that enhances general health. Remember never to give away personal power by allowing anyone else to interfere with the integrity of your assemblage point.

LEFT: The assemblage point, a vortex of energy (see page 116), allows an unending flow of energy, shaped like a figure eight, through our auric field. When the assemblage point is displaced, it results in illness or even death.

LEFT: Try to sense your friend's assemblage point, a vortex of energies usually located near the center of the chest or back.

117

Healing our bodies of light

Within this book, we have already looked at color in the chakras. However, our real journey is to explore ways in which we can reeducate ourselves and become more receptive to the color spectrum of light in all its manifestations, from the visually obvious to inner enlightenment. We are open to life when we do this, treading a path toward peace and deep contentment. Our flow of pranic life-force will be enhanced, and innate self-healing ability will be restored to its natural function.

The crystal computer

The aura may be seen as part of an other-worldly crystal computer. When fully functioning, it receives transmission of divine golden-white light, split into color messages, sending it through the chakras. Therefore, the maintenance of our chakras and the degree of color and hue passing through them are essential to the health and well-being of our physical body, for light is life.

It is widely accepted that the complex process of human evolution is not confined to a Darwinian model of change through eons of time. Many people consider that even now we are evolving exponentially, and that the next stage, restructuring our two-strand double-helix DNA into a 12-strand double-helix, has already begun. Understanding chakras and light takes us on an evolutionary leap to a new vision of health that is not based on diagnosis and treatment, but on fully living our inner truths through personal growth and healing.

Central to this process is trusting that we are always given what we need in our current lifetime—the joys and the pain. We are born into "original blessing," with potential to retain clarity and integrity through our chakras even if the physical body is pushed to its limits through aging. We could describe this process in computer jargon: throughout life we store information on the hard drive (physical body), then, at the point of death, transfer the entire memory onto a floppy disk (our chakras, particularly the soul star chakra), which we take with us on returning to our cosmic light body.

THE POWER OF LOVE

The power of love could prove to be the single most powerful act you can make to assist in self-healing. Wherever there is pain or discomfort, place your hand upon the area and think of love. Medical research has proved that if positive thought is directed to parts of the body, blood flow increases and healing processes are initiated through enhanced circulation. In addition, circulate unconditional love by drawing it into your body, with each breath, from whatever you feel is the source of divine love. Focus intently on your hands. As they become warm, you will know that unconditional love is being passed into the area of discomfort. Never think of any part of your body as a nuisance because this is not healthy—instead give praise for its marvellous intricacy, and direct love to it.

UNDERSTANDING CAUSES OF DIS-EASE

In a technological Western-style life, increasing numbers of people are separated from the world of nature. Responsibility for our bodies is largely relinquished to medical intervention and artificial drugs designed to target specific issues, frequently with detrimental side-effects. This may be acceptable in life-or-death situations, but many unnecessary prescribed-drug dependencies are created. We are now waking up to empower-ment through a preventative holistic approach to healthcare that tackles dis-ease (uneasiness of the body) as well as physical disease. Chakras, body, and mind are irrevocably interrelated. Our choice is to approach dis-ease in a different way, and a positive attitude is vital.

Diabetes may be an indication that sweetness or love in life is unbalanced. Often the emotion of love can be overprotective or smothering, as from mother to child. In addition to medical care, regular whole-body chakra balancing will be necessary to help ease this complaint.

RIGHT: *A holistic approach to life is based on the premise that the physical body, the mind, and the spirit are interdependent.*

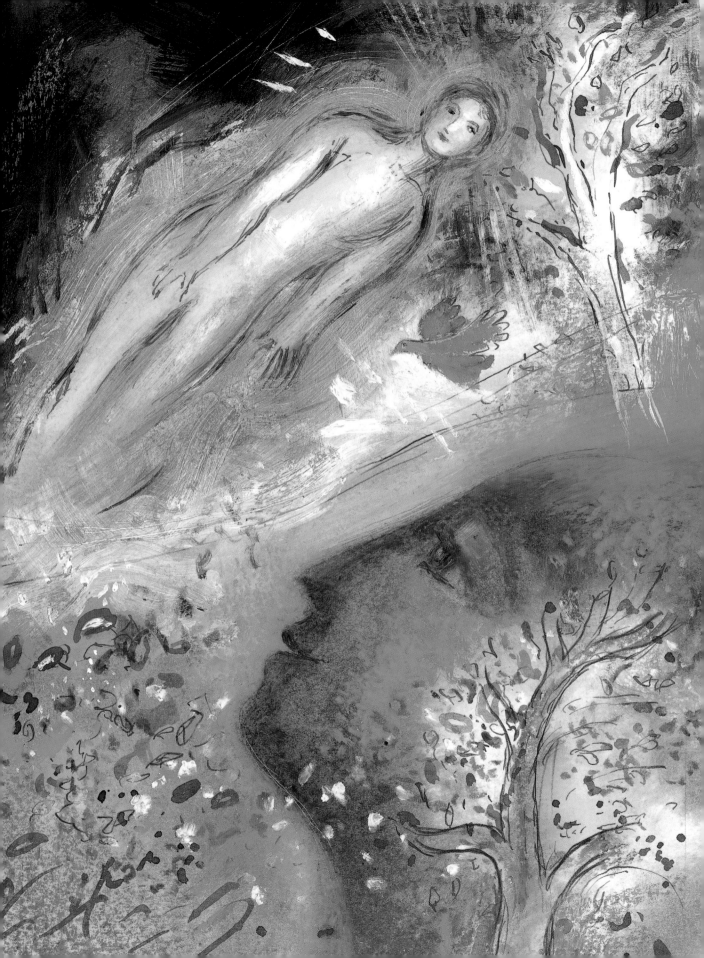

Taking responsibility

First, consider what is going wrong with the area of the body that is adversely affected, and what the implications of the dis-ease are. Explore the functions of associated chakra areas, particularly referring to pages 14 and 18. For example, developing gynecological or breast cancers may be closely linked to the feelings that a mother has when her children leave home. Her life had centered on the family, but now alternative interests are desperately required to move the emphasis of her energies from sacral and heart chakras on to another level of understanding and into a time of personal spiritual growth.

Second, consider when the illness or dis-ease first manifested itself—what was happening at that time, and up to two years prior to it? Is it a recurring condition? Or has a similar pattern, but different dis-ease, previously occurred in the person, family members, or friends? Remember, too, that sometimes being unwell is just the letting go of old patterns. Dis-ease may take a long time to penetrate the defenses of our aura and chakras, before coming to rest in the physical body. Because some time may elapse before natural holistic therapies clear dis-ease from the body and back out through the aura and chakras, be prepared to work on personal emotional issues that may be the actual "message" of the dis-ease.

THE MESSAGE OF DIS-EASE AND BODY-MIND CONNECTIONS TO CHAKRAS

There is an incredible connection between the mind and body. With our body we express conscious thoughts and feelings through movement and action. It is also the mirror of unconscious energies underlying everything we do. Complex physical systems convey messages from mind to body, but remember they are complemented by the intricacies of our chakras. We are an interface of vast converging possibilities. It is no wonder that our body sometimes balks at the immensity of the task. Yet there is a need to ask what the message of this dis-ease in our body is. Every part of the body has a different message to give. We may say, "I have to shoulder a lot of responsibility", or, "I am fed up to the back teeth." Take a look at the body language of a person who says these things. Are the shoulders hunched under the responsibility, or is the jaw locked with a habitual grinding of teeth to keep despair firmly within?

There are many examples of body messages—here are just a few:

• **Leg tension and circulation problems:** These suggest holding on, a lack of security, and disconnection with the Earth. Work on the Earth star chakra is needed.

• **Kidney problems:** The adrenal glands linked to the kidneys respond to stress levels. The sacral chakra requires balancing and stress factors reducing.

• **Bronchitis:** Inflammation of the bronchi suggests repressed anger, the need to "get it off your chest." Heart chakra work may help to release the problem and improve breathing.

• **Fibrositis or arthritis:** Pain or stiffness of the muscles or joints may indicate that mental attitudes are rigid and there is a consequent stagnation of energy flow through the limbs. Work generally with the heart chakra to encourage self-love, and also on the chakras nearest to the seat of the problem.

• **Migraine headaches:** May result from reduced supply of oxygen to the brain (although can be food related), suggesting that deeply held needs are being thwarted, or there is an overload of responsibility that denies fulfillment in a given area. Balancing the whole chakra system will help, together with heart chakra (self-worth), throat chakra (self-expression), and brow chakra (visualization of a goal) development.

HARMONIZING ELEMENTAL ENERGIES

A human lives on the planet, but a hue-man or hue-wo-man consciously lives as a being of light. This enhances certain rhythms of life, giving a perception of life within a greater

A stiff neck may indicate that you are limiting yourself by wanting to look only in one direction—work on the throat and brow chakras, together with the base chakra, to give increased energy levels and repattern the effects of limitation.

whole, in order that all humanity continues to evolve. Rhythms of life are governed by elemental nature manifesting in the four forms of Fire, Air, Water, and Earth. We cannot live without our Fire (prana/electrical/nerve) energy for more than three seconds. The solar plexus chakra helps store this energy. Our brain needs a constant supply of oxygen, which comes from Air. The heart chakra facilitates the movement of air. Without Water we cannot live for more than about 11 days. The sacral chakra focuses this function. We cannot survive without the Earth element—food—for more than approximately 56 days. The base chakra is the root of this function.

The element of Earth, representing growth and seeding, is associated with the base chakra. It is strongly linked with Water at the sacral chakra. Every seed first needs water in order to grow; a developing fetus is similar in that the child (seed) floats in a watery fluid. This gives an ideal opportunity for the embryonic chakras to grow within the mother's body. Fire, represented by prana, is focused at the solar plexus chakra and fueled by Air at the heart chakra. From the above points we are able to see that:

- The first four major chakras negotiate between each other.
- The same is true of the throat chakra, which attracts Ether, and the brow and crown chakras, which draw in the basic or elemental type of Spirit needed within the body.
- Our body needs all the nature elements on a straightforward physical level, and our chakras need the same elements on subtle spiritual levels.

THE SEVEN SEALS

In some chakra teachings, the elements are regarded as the first four "seals" covering or guarding the chakras on the cosmic tree of life. By practicing rigorous breathing and yoga, it is possible to open all seven seals simultaneously, and to access the higher self in the finest outer bodies of the aura. This action forms the light

body (a greatly enlarged auric field) as a geometrically shaped etheric star tetrahedron of light. When this occurs, the different qualities of light flowing through each seal are tremendously enhanced. The person becomes illuminated with an almost unreal presence, rarely seen except in great spiritual beings both past and present. Through the star tetrahedron numerous fantastic natural powers may be accessed. The yogis of old described them as *siddhis*.

Such enlightened beings go beyond obtaining their sustenance from the four elements and are able to take on another kind of food, that of pure energy, as nourishment. Their charisma is so strong that it is sufficient just to be in their presence or to gaze at their photograph in order for their inherent purity to be both transmitted and absorbed.

Yet the strongly kept secret running throughout major religious teachings is that we all have the potential to cleanse, nourish, and activate energy within our physical and subtle bodies. We can all take the first steps on this journey of enlightenment through the chakras, enjoying improved health as well as increased vitality in the process. Chakra awareness opens us to full potential as a hue-man or hue-wo-man in the "Age of Light" transition of the Earth and her peoples.

The siddhis (or powers) described in yoga literature are as follows: To be as minute as an atom; to increase in size at will; to negate gravity; to be in any place at will; to have any wish fulfilled; to control the energies of nature; to attain supreme self-control; to stop all desires; knowledge of past, present, and future lives; knowledge of the stars, the interior of the body, and mind; lightness and levitation; control of material elements and our senses; perfection and strength of the body. Surprisingly, these powers are considered to be temptations along the path of yoga.

ABOVE: *The star tetrahedron symbolizes miraculous powers gained through meditation.*

CLEAR GOLDEN-WHITE LIGHT
FROM CREATION ABOVE

INDIGO ENERGY FROM
THE NIGHT SKY ABOVE

TURQUOISE ENERGY FROM
THE DAYTIME SKY ABOVE

YELLOW ENERGY FROM
THE SUN ABOVE

GREEN ENERGY
HORIZONTALLY FROM TREES

ORANGE ENERGY
FROM THE EARTH BELOW

RED ENERGY FROM
THE EARTH BELOW

*As you breathe deeply you can visualize these directions
for the different colors entering the chakra seals.*

BREATHING EXERCISE TO OPEN THE SEVEN SEALS WITH COLOR

This is an immensely revitalizing breathing exercise that can be done anywhere, but preferably outside, in the early morning. It is important to keep your eyes open and focus on natural colors while doing this, and to breathe as deeply as you can manage. You may also choose to move around dynamically.

1 Stand, recalling the color sequence of the chakras as they ascend around the body. Imagine them as little spiral seals that are going to be empowered as you do color breathing for each one.

2 Bend down to touch the ground with your fingertips. Acknowledge the life-giving element of Earth, and breathe in the color red. Do this for three breaths, saturating the whole of your legs and base chakra with it.

3 Begin to stand up, lifting your hands slowly in front of your legs, resting them just below your navel, simultaneously breathing in orange for three breaths.

4 Bring your hands to your solar plexus and breathe in bright yellow for three breaths.

5 Open your arms wide, breathing in the bright green of grass and trees. Using your arms and hands, pull this into your chest and heart chakra in three breaths.

6 Move your hands to throat chakra level, changing the color of the three breaths to turquoise.

7 Turn the palms of your hands outward, touching the tips of the thumbs and forefingers together—making a triangular pyramid shape—and holding it before your brow chakra. Take three breaths of deep sky-blue.

8 Move the pyramid shape above your head. Breathe in three breaths of violet.

9 Finally, stretch your arms straight up high above your head, reaching for clear, golden-white light, and take three breaths. Draw your hands down in front of your body, taking just one breath now for every chakra, of appropriate color, resealing each with a little spiral of color.

10 Touch the ground with the fingertips of both hands.

Note: Once you have used this deep-breathing exercise regularly for 28 days, increase the number of breaths in each case from three to seven.

Old and new ways of healing and balancing chakras

Human consciousness is constantly changing. The following chakra balancing methods can be studied, or experienced with a practitioner.

REIKI

Reiki is universal love, unconditionally received and given. Modern practitioners receive information in three stages of "attunements." Reiki has been understood since very early times, and practiced by the Essenes and some orders of Buddhists. It was rediscovered in the late 1800s by Mikao Usui, while on a three-week period of meditation on Mount Koriyama in Japan. He was given a vision of the lost secret symbols used in Reiki healing. Reiki allows a powerful flow of specific pranic energy, differentiated as universal love, to pass through the healer's hands while they are placed to benefit the recipient's aura and chakras, or body. When giving Reiki, it is not necessary to know the other person's symptoms. After receiving a Reiki 1 attunement you can give self-healing, which benefits your own chakras.

HANDS-ON HEALING

Hands-on or spiritual healing is well known in Britain. Spiritualist churches and a number of healing federations provide training, usually as a two-year certificated course. A certificated healer is able to obtain insurance to practice and be accepted for work in some hospitals.

RADIONICS

Radionics, developed more than one hundred years ago from the work of theosophist Alice Bailey, is based upon unity, our wholeness, and sharing a common ground with all life-forms. The electromagnetic energy field of the Earth, in which we are all immersed, as well as our own electromagnetic auric field, indicates the ways in which we can heal, for all is energy. Radionics uses instruments in the diagnosis and transmission of the energies/inner processes involved. Practitioners also use a form of dowsing called radiesthesia (a type of ESP). They determine the balance and flow of the chakras, subtle bodies, and organ systems and, together with spiritual psychology, produce a life-pattern that effects change in the recipient. Because radionics utilizes the Earth's energy field, treatment is often given from a distance and can be used on any living system such as a human being, an animal, a plant, or the soil.

GEM ELIXIRS AND FLOWER ESSENCES

There is a sympathetic association between gem elixirs and flower essences, and the chakras. Both are methods of vibrational healing. Recent channeled guidance is unlocking wisdom teachings associated with these essences, which appear to have origins in ancient Lemuria and Atlantis. Gem elixirs, often prepared homeopathically, come from inorganic material. This makes them valuable for use on the physical symptoms of chakra imbalance. Treatment can then be followed by the appropriate flower essences, because these come from plants that have a much higher concentration of life's force. They remove the remaining toxicities from the body and help deal with emotional issues. Flower essences are a living vehicle that hold the pattern of consciousness, while crystals or gems amplify consciousness. There are many ranges of flower essences available today, but consult a qualified practitioner for the best results.

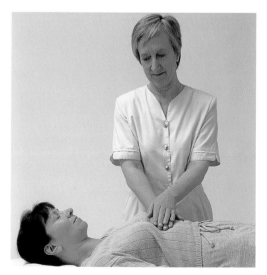

ABOVE: *Hands-on healers are trained to understand the chakras and auras, and become practiced at balancing them.*

HOW TO MAKE A SIMPLE GEM/ CRYSTAL ELIXIR

Choose a tumbled stone or crystal to balance the chakra in question. Ensure that it is hard, not water-soluble, and does not have any poisonous or metallic qualities. If in doubt use clear quartz, because it has the effect of balancing all the chakras.
1. Cleanse the crystal first.
2. Place it in a plain glass of pure spring water, cover with a sheet of white paper or clear glass, and leave in the sunshine (or daylight) for approximately three hours. The water will become encoded with the energies of the crystalline vibration.
3. Remove the crystal and slowly sip the water.

Caution: you should never ingest crushed crystal.

ABOVE: *Essential oils are extracted from tiny sacs of fragrance stored inside plants. They contain many natural, healing chemicals.*

RIGHT: *Anointing the brow chakra. Massage in a spiraling motion, moving outward from the center.*

ESSENTIAL AROMATIC PLANT OILS

Used in aromatherapy, essential oils are the distilled living essence of plants or flowers. A qualified aromatherapist should be aware of chakras as well as physical body needs when choosing appropriate oils (which are mixed with a carrier oil) for massage purposes. The charts in Chapter 3 give suggested essential oils for each chakra.

ANOINTING THE CHAKRAS WITH ESSENTIAL OILS

This is a beautiful thing to do either for yourself or for an intimate friend. If you can afford only one essential oil, choose a good-quality natural rose or lavender oil. A "carrier" oil is required to dilute the extremely concentrated essential oil. You can use almond, grapeseed, or even pure sunflower cooking oil. Pour a teaspoonful of carrier oil into a saucer. Add just one or two drops (maximum) of essential oil. The following instructions are for when working with a friend.

1 Sit quietly, or go through the relaxation exercise together, until you feel very calm.
2 "Tune in" to the energies of both your own and your friend's chakras, one at a time. Observe how your chakras are reacting.
3 Locate the chakras on your friend's body. Sensing the appropriate direction, gently massage each with oil in a circling motion, within a 2–6in (5–15cm) diameter.

THE MEDICINE WHEEL

Indigenous peoples of the Americas use a medicine wheel as a symbolic tool to associate with their connection to all life. Its teachings are very old, wise ways of effecting healing, which have been passed down orally through the generations. These teachings include references to centers of power—the chakras. The main ways of healing are through ceremony, ritual, prayer, and the use of traditional herbs. The idea of balance in all things is central to medicine wheel teachings.

DOORWAYS AND PORTALS

Traditionally, chakras are activated in sequence from the base to the crown. But human consciousness is expanding, life seems to be speeding up, and experiences follow quickly, one upon the other. More people are prepared to consider that they are not just a physical body. The medicine of the future is preventative healthcare based on energy flows and vibrational frequencies.

Having studied chakras individually, we have now reached the point of considering all the chakras as a whole interrelated organization. They may be opened simultaneously as doorways or portals of opportunity to a new perspective of health. When star knowledge is applied to the chakras as portals, it is helpful to visualize them as brilliantly colored crystalline lenses receiving information encoded from stars throughout the cosmos. Little is understood about the true nature of this high-vibration energy, except that our whole solar system is "bathed" in it. The potent energy is received here on Earth via our Sun and planetary system, which act as immense crystal lenses to transmute it into a form capable of being channeled by chakras and assimilated by our bodies.

GIVING A CHAKRA CRYSTAL "SHOWER"

An excellent way to tone up a friend's chakras is to use a large, clear, quartz crystal point, held along its length, so that you direct one of the long sides during the "shower." Ask your friend to stand in the middle of the room and, if possible, use a smudge stick or incense to create a sacred circular space around him or her. Next visualize this as a circle of light, and step into it. You will have already cleansed and dedicated your quartz crystal.

Hold the point and the largest face of the crystal tip on your partner's spiritual grounding point. This is midway between the heart and solar plexus chakras, over the sternum. Place your hand on your friend's back so that you can feel the crystal ray as it passes through the body and clothes. This will make all the chakras receptive. Now, stand a little in front of your friend and, using the long side of the crystal, move it down within the auric field. Begin just above the head, moving down the center front of the body, and then down one leg to touch the ground. Repeat by beginning above the head, moving down the center front of the body and onward through the other leg, again touching the ground. Then repeat these two actions down the back of the body. The cleansing effect is like a powerful crystal shower, drawing away any positive ions that have accumulated in the electromagnetic field of the aura, and discharging them into the ground. It will bring the chakras into alignment and balance.

Finish by pointing and moving the crystal in a large figure eight pattern, both in front of and behind the person, to close the chakras to a comfortable level and to protect the aura.

THE CHAKRA FLOWER

We tend the "garden" of Spirit whenever our chakras begin to open, and as we strengthen our resolve to grow toward the light. Like sunflowers that follow the course of the Sun across the sky, we instinctively turn to light and move away from darkness. Relaxation, visualization, and meditation are the fertile ground of our mind, and creativity is the nourishing "food" that encourages the flowering of our chakras. We are limitless beings of light, vehicles for the pure expression of unconditional love. Nothing can stop us from achieving our full potential, if it is our intention to grow.

Use this book with lightness and love in your heart chakra, expanding the wisdom acquired through the insight of the third eye. Experience how wisdom is of a different nature from knowledge, for knowledge is obtained through the outer eyes only. But with the third eye, visionary consciousness dawns. Allow the movement of full joyful expression from the base and sacral chakras, and sing out through your throat chakra. Affirm: "Life, love, laughter—yet be still and placid within."

Look with the opened inner eye. You will see everything you need, waiting to be shared.

ABOVE: *Open the door to the fragrant garden of the Spirit. Take steps to walk among its flowers.*

LEFT: *The crystal shower. Feel the chakras become receptive as you hold the crystal between the heart and solar plexus.*

Further reading

GENERAL
The Raiment of Light
David Tansley
Arkana 1985

16 Steps to Health and Energy
Pauline Wills and Theo Gimbel
Llewellyn 1992

Wheels of Light
Rosalyn L. Bruyere
Simon and Schuster 1994

The Bodymind Workbook
Debbie Shapiro
Element 1997

Vibrational Medicine
Richard Gerber M.D.
Bear and Co. 1988

Where Science and Magic Meet
Serena Roney-Dougal
Element 1995

Pi in the Sky
Michael Poynder
Rider 1992

Bringers of the Dawn
Barbara Marciniak
Bear and Co. 1992

Chakra Handbook
Sharamon and Baginski
Lotus Light 1996

The Bhagavad-Gita
translated by Maharishi Mahesh Yogi
Penguin 1969

YOGA
Light on Yoga
B.K.S. Iyengar
Unwin 1976

Hathapradipika
Kevin and Venika Kingsland
Grael Comm. 1977

COLOR
Color
Rudolf Steiner
Rudolf Steiner Press 1992

Color Therapy Workbook
Theo Gimbel
Element 1993

The Power of the Rays
S.G.J. Ouseley
Fowler 1951

SOUND
Sounding the Inner Landscape
Kay Gardener
Element 1997

WATER
Living Water: Viktor Schauberger and the Secrets of Natural Energy
Olof Alexandersson
Gateway Books 1990

RADIONICS
Chakras, Rays, and Radionics
David Tansley
C.W. Daniel 1992

CRYSTALS
The Power of Gems and Crystals
Soozi Holbeche
Piatkus 1989

American Indian Secrets of Crystal Healing
Luc Bourgault
Foulsham 1997

HEALING
Hands of Light
Barbara Ann Brennan
Bantam Doubleday 1990

Essential Reiki
Diane Stein
Crossing Press 1995

Index

Picture credits

The publishers are grateful to the following for permission to reproduce copyright material:

Anthroposophical Society in Great Britain: p. 30T.
Art Archive: pp. 2, 10T, 19, 116.
A–Z Botanical Collection: p. 17B.
Bridgeman Art Library: pp. 49B, Private Collection; 60, Victoria & Albert Museum; 65, Chartres Cathedral; 67, Louvre; 83, Chester Beatty Library & Gallery of Oriental Art.
Elizabeth Whiting & Associates: p. 68T.
Fortean Picture Library: pp. 95T, 99T, 111T&B.
Garden Picture Library: pp. 47, 55, 125T.
Sarah Howerd: p. 57T.
Hutchison Library: pp. 20, 37B, 41, 53B, 79, 80BR, 82T, 85, 88.
Image Bank: pp. 8B, 12, 34, 36, 38B, 39, 40, 43, 44, 48BR, 51, 54, 57B, 59, 61B, 62, 63, 75C, 86B, 92L, 93B, 100, 121.
Lucis Trust: p. 74T.
Rex Features: p. 52.
Ben Rogerson: p. 80BL.
Science Photo Library: pp. 7, 45T, 101.
Margaret Stamp: p. 13T.
Stock Market: pp. 27T, 31T, 56B.
Tibet Images: p. 33TL.
Tony Stone Images: pp. 75T&B, 82L, 91.

Many thanks to the Green Man Bookshop and Gallery, 24 South Street, Eastbourne, East Sussex, UK, for the loan of the chalice on page 33.

Author's acknowledgments

To everyone who has enriched my life journey by enhancing my understanding of the Light, including Barbara Griggs, Friends of Yoga; Theophilus Gimbel DCE, Hygeia College of Colour; Stephanie Harrison, International College of Crystal Healing; Michael Walker, Spiritual Teacher; Pamela Yeend, Artist; Alan Norsworthy, Reiki Master; and my many Yoga, Crystal Healing, Shamanic, and Color students in the UK. Special thanks to Pauline Wills, Oracle School of Colour, who encouraged me while I was writing this book and Michael F. Baker, my husband and Sound and Color Healer, for his unique inspirations and patient correction of text. Lastly thanks to the plants, trees, crystals, and natural world that I communicate with every day and the ancient indigenous wisdom of the Maya elders of Central America.